The Phantom Empire

The Phantom Empire

Geoffrey O'Brien

W. W. Norton & Company
New York · London

Some of the material in this book appeared previously, in
different form, in *The New York Review of Books*, *The Village Voice*,
and *New Observations*. Of many sources consulted, I am
particularly indebted to the historical researches of Charles
Musser, Kevin Brownlow, and Noel Burch.

Copyright © 1993 by Geoffrey O'Brien
All rights reserved
Printed in the United States of America
First Edition

The text of this book is composed in 12/15 Perpetua
with the display set in Corvinus Skyline.
Composition and manufacturing by The Haddon Craftsmen, Inc.
Book design by Chris Welch

Library of Congress Cataloging-in-Publication Data
O'Brien, Geoffrey, 1948–
    The phantom empire / by Geoffrey O'Brien.
        p.   cm.
    Includes index.
    1. Motion pictures—Psychological aspects.   I. Title.
PN1995.O17   1993
791.43'01'3—dc20   93-6824

ISBN 0-393-03549-2
W. W. Norton & Company, Inc., 500 Fifth Avenue
New York, N.Y. 10110
W. W. Norton & Company Ltd., 10 Coptic Street
London WC1A 1PU
1 2 3 4 5 6 7 8 9 0

This book is for Heather

contents

list of illustrations

It seems I've always slept,
Since, if I've dreamed what I've just seen and heard
Palpably and for certain, then I am dreaming
What I see now—nor is it strange I'm tired,
Since what I, sleeping, see, tells me that I
Was dreaming when I thought I was awake.
—PEDRO CALDERÓN DE LA BARCA, *LA VIDA ES SUENO*
   (TRANS. ROY CAMPBELL)

But when the last flicker of the last picture in a reel had faded away, when the lights in the auditorium went up, and the field of vision stood revealed as an empty sheet of canvas, there was not even applause. Nobody was there to be applauded, to be called before the curtain and thanked for the rendition. The actors who had assembled to present the scenes they had just enjoyed were scattered to the winds; only their shadows had been here. . . .
—THOMAS MANN, *THE MAGIC MOUNTAIN*

Just keep saying to yourself: ''It's only a movie. . . . It's only a movie. . . . It's only a movie. . . .''
—ADVERTISEMENT FOR *STRAIT-JACKET* (1964)

mister memory

Establishing shot: dark city, late modern period.

The camera rolls through the street. Shiny fog effect. They smear the props with jelly to make them gleam. Or something. They have tricks, they've studied human perception. Their lab technicians know exactly what makes people stare or look away, and for how long. They have perfected a science of blinks.

The visual team steers the lens past the strategically placed heaps of urban debris. They tilt the lights so the fetid greenish pools in the gutter glitter more stylishly. The camera plows ahead as if the spectator were perched on top of a bullet train or strapped on board a roller coaster. A ride is being manufactured. The wind machine blows the piles of newspaper and cardboard around in the fog. An animal trainer was employed to make the rat scamper from the alley mouth at precisely the moment when the camera skids through the pool to ensure an artistic splash at the frame's edge.

Now the camera slows down a little, so the spectator has more time to see what's going on. The art director had the extras made up to look exactly like the junkies on Avenue C. He did research on graffiti and broken doorknobs. The poverty is totally convincing. Did the actors voluntarily starve themselves, and go on a steady diet of Twinkies and methadone, out of their desire to break into the movies? It stutters along, stopping and starting, to let each face hold the screen for a beat so the spectator can read the image and distinguish it from its neighbors: this one has a gold tooth . . . this one has no teeth . . . this one is terminally jaundiced . . . this one flashes a cannibalistic grin . . . this one has an eroded remnant of waif-like pathos . . . the muscles of this one were perfected in stir . . . this one (the camera holds him longer so he can function as punch line) points accusingly at the camera like a warlock threatening vengeance on his persecutors.

But the camera escapes effortlessly from the creatures. It can go wherever it wants to go, scattering images of city without ever having to inhabit any of them. It prowls through one narrow alley after another, through places defined by the absence of spectators. The bass chords on the Dolby soundtrack make them sound like places where no spectator would ever want to be.

It brushes muck aside, burrows among heaps of bones. Stray cats pounce howling past its lens. It creeps up a wall. Over the Dolby bass a synthesized flutelike rasping—a suppressed asthmatic moan—is superimposed. It keeps climbing the wall, slowing the action down, stretching it out to let the irritating insistence of the flutelike rasping get under the skin.

The camera has found what it was looking for: the blinds of an apartment. After hanging outside the window long enough to show that it's a window, it glides effortlessly through the security gates, through the glass, and sails across . . .

. . . a large cluttered space, a paneled-wood high-tech wasteland littered with cassettes and canisters and TV monitors. Everything is the latest model but somehow dusty, battered, worn out before its time, like the artifacts in *Blade Runner* and *The Road Warrior*. The space is lit by the glow of a single television screen.

The forward movement continues—a voluptuously prolonged Steadicam journey across the interior landscape—toward its inexorable destination: an oddly immobile body propped up on a couch. This is the spectator. The camera zeroes in until the screen fills with a close-up of a closed eyelid, an eyelid shown in such microscopic detail that its tremor (indicative of an REM state) takes on the epic scale of prairie schooners crossing the wide Missouri or of Russian sailors rising up to slaughter their officers.

As if startled by an unpleasant dream, the lid pops open: a sudden view of a liquid abyss, like the deep well in the fortress where the lost jewel is hidden in *Moonfleet*. The open eye resembles an alien life form only partly distinguishable—to an innocent astronaut's gaze—from the landscape of its planet.

The figure on the couch is you. You have woken up in the middle of your life to find yourself alone in what for a second you take to be a movie theater. It seems to be 2 A.M. of a

summer night toward the end of the twentieth century. The
city emits a steady rattle of traffic noise and air conditioning, a
hum as monolithic as silence. The crackheads cluster for asy-
lum under the peep show's awning. Bass patterns from cruis-
ing radios provide accompaniment for a solitary car alarm.

The cable channel was left on. In *The Four Feathers* Ralph
Richardson is going blind again. The Miklos Rozsa soundtrack
underscores the cruel process by which—as Richardson peers
intently through field glasses, on the lookout for the approaching army of Mahdist fanatics—his pith helmet rolls beyond
reach down the rocks into the Sudanese desert. He will be
stuck on that exposed ledge until the optic nerve burns away.

What you thought was a movie theater turns out to be
home.

A peculiar sort of home, though, more like a receiving
station: an aptly named "studio apartment" combining the
functions of screening room, recording studio, and small-scale
archive. The Museum of Everything, crammed with posters,
postcards, cassettes, laser discs, soundtrack albums, books of
movie stills. Home finally is wherever the movie is playing, a
pup tent that can go up wherever there's a plug for the Home
Entertainment Center. A wired clearing in the jungle, guarded
by radar, where off-duty soldiers are permitted to forget
where they are for a while.

THE FOUR FEATHERS, in this space, functions as mental
wallpaper. You've seen it—inhabited it—that often. It seems
like something that must have happened to you personally
once. You were a young man from a distinguished military

family with the horrifying suspicion that you lacked the courage to be a warrior. Your childhood was blighted by that suspicion, as night after night you walked up to bed past a long row of heroic ancestors. So when all your chums joined up to go to the Sudan with Kitchener's expedition you backed off, resigned your commission. You said it was because you were in love with your fiancée Ethne and wanted only to settle down to a life of rural gentility in her company—you even ventured to suggest that you had some serious problems with the government's imperial policies—but you knew deep down that wasn't the real reason. The situation became untenable when your three friends gave you a little box containing three white feathers denoting cowardice; and when Ethne herself made it only too obvious that she too had lost faith in you, you plucked a plume out of her fan, making it Four Feathers.

So you disappeared into Egypt. You worked as a laborer hauling dhows along the Nile, disguising yourself as a Zingari tribesman because all the members of that tribe had had their tongues cut out and you would therefore not have to communicate in Arabic. And everything happened as ordained: the ritual was carried out correctly and appropriately. You suffered hunger and thirst. You were beaten, humiliated, imprisoned, universally despised, all as a necessary prelude to saving your fickle friends and the British Empire along with them. You showed them.

You showed them so well that your humiliation was somehow deflected to Ralph Richardson, one of the three who had given you the white feather in the first place. His punishment was to go blind, to lose Ethne's love (even though she would have gone through with the marriage for form's sake), finally

to make the grand gesture of withdrawing from the engage-
ment by pretending that he had to go to Germany for eye
surgery. In that ballet of self-sacrifice, Richardson was given
the finest moment, demonstrating that he had learned Braille
by reading from *The Tempest:*

> *The isle is full of noises,*
> *Sounds and sweet airs, that give delight, and hurt not.*
> *Sometimes a thousand twangling instruments*
> *Will hum about mine ears.*

But Braille would make it too easy on him, too much like a
free ride; to make it perfect he had to acknowledge that he'd
known the passage by heart since his school days.

What fate decreed that your consciousness should be preoccupied, even fleetingly, with a 1939 Alexander Korda production based on a novel written by A.E.W. Mason in 1902, and
filmed at least three times in the silent era and three times
more after the advent of talkies, most recently as a made-for-
TV movie starring Beau Bridges in 1977? And what sort of
knowledge had you acquired by contemplating those transfor-
mations?

A.E.W. Mason had been about twenty in 1885 when the
Mahdi's religiously inspired warriors overran the defenses of
Khartoum and slaughtered "Chinese" Gordon. (That pivotal
event, depicted only cursorily in *The Four Feathers,* would have
to wait until the 1966 *Khartoum* for its first, and perhaps last,
full-scale cinematic representation.) As his nickname indicated, Gordon's military successes in capturing Peking and
suppressing the Taiping Rebellion had already turned him into

something like a fictional character, perhaps already as exotic to Mason as he would be to later generations. Certainly the Mahdi, a carpenter's son turned religious prophet whose spontaneously recruited armies had rapidly overrun the Sudan, must have seemed unimaginably exotic.

Probably A.E.W. Mason did not, at age twenty, realize that he would eventually write a best-selling novel set in the territory over which the Mahdi had asserted his spiritual and temporal authority. Almost certainly he did not realize that that novel would be made into a movie six times over, if he was even more than marginally aware, in 1902, that movies existed. The Mahdi and General Gordon are equally unlikely to have contemplated the idea that their destinies—which they doubtless conceived exclusively in religious or geopolitical terms—would come to exist in an independent fictional sphere, providing the premise for an immensely popular novel which would in turn be recycled repeatedly in a medium that would not emerge for another decade after Gordon's death.

(For that matter, neither the Mahdi nor Gordon, farseeing as they may have been, are likely to have imagined that less than a hundred years after the events at Khartoum, they would be portrayed in an internationally distributed ''road show'' movie by Laurence Olivier and Charlton Heston respectively. Even less could they have foreseen that an Englishman, Laurence Olivier, would feel an artistic obligation to study Arabic pronunciation sufficiently to create a lifelike mimicry; or that by 1966, the year of *Khartoum*'s release, a British production would find it necessary for box-office reasons to cast an American in the role of General Gordon.)

But however little they knew what lay ahead, you as spectator know even less of where you come from. The Sudanese question, or the very existence of the Sudan: how likely is it you would have even a glimmer of them without the cultural accidents of *The Four Feathers* and *Khartoum*? Khartoum and Omdurman are old news events accidentally preserved in movie plots, like the mammoths and saber-toothed tigers caught in the La Brea tar pits. For that matter isn't the British Empire by now remembered chiefly as the occasion for Alexander Korda movies, for C. Aubrey Smith's priceless impressions of blustery colonels and old India hands, for *Sanders of the River* and *Gunga Din* and *The Charge of the Light Brigade*?

At the time of the battle of Omdurman in 1898, when Kitchener led his Anglo-Egyptian force to victory against the Khalifa (who had succeeded to power in the Sudan following the Mahdi's untimely death), A.E.W. Mason was thirty-three years old. Did he by this point already have a glimmer of the novel he would publish four years later, or did Kitchener's coup set the whole thing off in a sudden burst of inspiration? Presumably Mason was a bit too old—or simply disinclined, like his hero Harry Feversham—to join up as a volunteer with the young men who marched with Kitchener against the black flag of the Khalifa.

Was it his absence from the desert battlefield that he managed to glorify through Harry's vicarious exploits? In any event he became, by writing *The Four Feathers,* as much a hero as if he had actually fought in the desert, appropriating an aura of valor by describing it. Thirty-four years later he would still be cheering the English on in *Fire over England,* a novel of the Spanish Armada that, filmed (again by Korda) in 1937, provided a nationalist rallying point in the face of impending Continental dangers.

BY 1902, WHEN *The Four Feathers* was published, outlets all over the British Isles were showing films under a variety of names: the Kinetoscope, the theatrograph, the animatograph. In 1905 the producer Cecil Hepworth released his epoch-making one-reel narrative *Rescued by Rover*. By the standards of the day it was a triumph of narrative complexity to depict the abduction of a baby by a gypsy, and the baby's subsequent rescue by a devoted dog. Film language reached a new plateau in the scene where Rover vainly (and silently) scratched and howled in his efforts to tell the baby's parents what was going on.

A.E.W. Mason may have begun to foresee dimly that his enormously popular story would be filmed, although it is hard to imagine him imagining that it would be remade, for the sixth time, seventy-five years after its initial publication, for a medium (television) well along in the process of supplanting the primitive medium (movies) just coming to birth when Mason wrote the universally appreciated story of Harry Feversham and those four white feathers.

Nothing could be more random than watching this particular movie made more than half a century earlier, a movie carefully designed to appeal to the tastes and prejudices of a vanished audience. But the process is arbitrary every step of the way: arbitrary for A.E.W. Mason to have written the book, for it to have been filmed six separate times, for the Korda brothers to have established (by making the definitive 1939 version) a fortuitous Hungarian-Sudanese connection under the unifying aegis of the British Empire, for the careers of thousands of actors, technicians, publicists, and other laborers to be enmeshed in this piece of intellectual property, not counting the millions sitting passively in the audience, each of them with a life in which it would be difficult to argue that *The Four Feathers* made much ultimate difference.

Not counting, either, the actual Sudanese whose history and landscape were plundered to make it all possible, and who may for a variety of reasons not have fully savored or even seen *The Four Feathers* in any of its avatars. A good number of those Sudanese, however, actually appeared in the Korda version at least, reenacting the charge of the Fuzzy Wuzzies in visual terms instantly recognizable to audiences reared on the poetry of Rudyard Kipling:

> So 'ere's to you, Fuzzy Wuzzy, at yer 'ome in the Sowdan;
> You're a pore benighted 'eathen, but a first-class fightin' man!

The sight of those Beja tribesmen—the single most memorable image in the movie—would have seemed to provide belated confirmation of the accuracy of Kipling's reporting.

The footage—*real* footage of *real* desert warriors—was to prove unexpectedly valuable when the game, interrupted by world war, was called on account of the passing of colonialism. The British were out of the Sudan by 1956, and after the fall of the Empire both the economics and the cultural politics of reenacting the Battle of Omdurman on location became considerably more problematic. Consequently those 1939 images would have to be reused again and again, surfacing twenty years later in the remake *Storm over the Nile* as if the image of the Sudan had been fixed once and for all.

Meanwhile there exist—at the very moment that you stare with half-open eye at the admirably luminous colors transmitted by the cable channel—a real Nile, a real Sudan, a real Omdurman. The bones of Kitchener and the Khalifa Abdullahi ibn Sayed Mohammed really exist somewhere on or in the earth, along with the bones of Ralph Richardson and June Duprez. It all really happened, the filming as much as the events that prompted it. The staging of the battle of Omdurman for *The Four Feathers* was as much a historical, certifiable event as the battle itself. You have the proof before you, the actual footage of the faked battle: and that is all you have, or can ever have.

IT'S IMPOSSIBLE TO linger on any moment or aspect of this historical flux. You're caught in the forward surge. Whatever muscle the brain employs to warehouse thoughts and perceptions is reduced to inadequate flailing gestures: "Have to make a note of that, if this thing ever stops moving for a second." But it doesn't. No memorization is occurring. Nothing repeats often enough. You pant helplessly after the tantalizing shifting shadows.

The Four Feathers already links up with a larger history than you could hope to grasp: but *The Four Feathers* is, after all, only one among an infinite number of such clusters of relationships. You can kill it in a second if you are tired of it, and all the straggling thoughts that accrue to it. If you no longer like that history, pick a different one. Plunge in anywhere. You're surrounded by mountains of potential images, boxes of cassettes sprawled in disorderly heaps. The world, ready to be activated at your whim.

It's all here: *The Cabinet of Dr. Caligari* and *The Battleship*

Potemkin, Charlie Chaplin in drag, Filipino horror movies about mad surgeons, animated maps tracking the pincer movements of Rommel's Panzer divisions, Egyptian soap operas in which insanely jealous husbands weep for what seems like hours at a stretch, made-for-TV stories about hitchhikers and serial killers, a long row of seventy-minute cavalry westerns, Russian science fiction intercut with nude scenes shot on Long Island, the best of the Bowery Boys, an amateur bondage cassette filmed on location in a dentist's office in Ronkonkoma, *They Drive by Night, All This and Heaven Too, The Barkleys of Broadway,* Hindi religious musicals, Japanese gangster movies, countless adaptations of the works of William Shakespeare, Charles Dickens, and the Brontë sisters, *L'Avventura, The Gene Krupa Story, Night of the Blind Dead,* Betty Boop cartoons with color added, touristic documentation of Calcutta and Isfahan, a Bulgarian punk band captured live, and the complete photoplays of Louise Brooks, Greta Garbo, and Veronica Lake.

So you hit the OFF button. Dead screen. But you cannot "stop" *The Four Feathers* by so crude a maneuver. It persists along with the ten thousand other select favorites, a colony of barnacles clinging to the underside of your visual memory. It's too late, or too soon, to turn off the images. You're already too involved, and it's way too early to be tired yet. They inhabit you, and tonight they feel like staying up maybe until first light.

The camera prowls around the room. This is how the eye works at the end of the twentieth century, after a hundred years of training. The camera slides through the doorway and feels its way like a blind man along the surface of the clutter: a von Sternberg shot, a *Citizen Kane* shot. The mind would like to move with that sensuous calm, to be the mechanical invulnerable eye passing disembodied through space, magnifying and illuminating at will, forcing the world to reveal itself. The surfaces flatten themselves into pictures as it goes by.

The field of vision wants to be filled. The eye hungers for compositions and camera movements, for chases and crashes, for sudden sprawling boom-shot vistas. Memory isn't enough. The boxes of cassettes hold more than memory: they hold the world, if only there were time to screen it all. They are home movies of the twentieth century. As a spectator you know those people intimately, Marlene Dietrich and Buster Keaton, Shirley Temple and Bruce Lee, Bela Lugosi and Carmen Miranda and Alan Ladd.

They have been your neighbors, your trenchmates, your guidance counselors, your steady dates. You wouldn't be surprised by anything that could ever have happened in their movies. You've seen it all, you saw the remake, you saw the original again twenty years later and found it hadn't changed at all. Not one twitch or crinkle of grin had altered. They live forever. Objectively, they don't give a damn about you.

The films get their hooks into you by propping up memory, or perhaps more accurately by substituting for memory. You can trace each image back to an original encounter; various rooms, theaters, even nations exist primarily as the place where a particular image first emerged. "Ankara is where I first saw *Pillow Talk*." More than anything the pictures serve as reminders of the people who watched them. That's the post-apocalyptic science-fiction movie about giant cockroaches in Los Angeles that so deeply and inexplicably disturbed Michael. That's the doomed starlet on whom Frieda modeled her youth. That's the sentimental wartime fantasy that Dave has spent his adult life attempting to reenact. That's the comedy that Patrick watched on Channel Nine the night before he jumped.

There were movies endured during all-night sieges of insomnia, movies left on while making love, movies clung to in the wake of disaster as a substitute for grieving. There were movies used as a focus point, to give the group something to laugh at or to dream about, or simply to allow them a brief respite from being so endlessly involved with one another. Once a roomful of students on mescaline mistook *Decision at Sundown* for a movie about Tibet and Randolph Scott for a solitary lamaistic ascetic, until someone muttered: "You see? Violence is just a metaphor for Dharma."

All those rooms were realer than the screen (the screen was a toy occupying a small corner of the real), but the screen has somehow outlived them. The false images survived the mortals who idly allowed their eyes to dwell on them. It gets so bad you end up searching an unchanging celluloid surface for a clue to vanished worlds, as if by starting up the movie the people who once watched it together would start up too. Ghosts summoned by ghosts. How often you've wished that memory could be as sharp, solid, and mechanical as a movie, that the mind could give way to remembering as effortlessly as the eye submits to the ritual glide of the camera on its tracks, accompanied by the offscreen adult voice of a superannuated child:

"The town has changed now and the familiar voices have gone still. . . . Seems like folks are in more of a hurry than they ever used to be. . . . But for me it will always be the way it was that day the stage brought the parson to town. . . ." Jingling of spurs, sprightly up-tempo motif, discreet suggestion of the bustle of everyday commerce. The camera would move forward into the past, poking into its seams and corners. If only it had been possible to live like this, to examine with such leisure all sides of things. The dead—each introduced by a humorous vignette—would set about their yard work and kitchen chores to the accompaniment of cunningly orchestrated twitters and clip-clops. The camera would have preserved them the way people preserve food, for sustenance in time of famine.

AT TWO IN the morning you have gone a bit blank. How many times have you known this empty wakefulness? *The Four Feathers* was on and you were there to watch it. It provided minimal proof that you were not dead. An observer from a more ancient tribal society would perhaps deduce that you had succumbed to death-in-life, the trance state in which (under the malign power of some untraceable sorcery) the soul goes walking and the body slumps uselessly like a puppet abandoned by its master. If he had been around the neighborhood long enough to study a little film history, that same observer might take you for one of the mind-controlled subjects of the invisible supercriminal Doctor Mabuse.

If Dana Andrews, for example, were to interrogate you under hypnosis, you might reply in a curiously toneless voice: "I am the living end product of a bizarre experiment. They have colonized my memory. I had a name once but I am no longer sure what it signifies. For the memories and images in my brain are shared by so many other people that we are almost interchangeable.'' And Andrews—stolid and inexorable in his trench coat, a bit hoarse from hours of questioning—would force the issue: "But who are you? Tell me who you are!" And with a shriek of thoroughly unconvincing hysterical laughter you would burst out: "I'm no one! I'm everyone! All by myself I'm an electronic crowd scene!"

You can plainly visualize how such a scene would be lit, and can savor the precise flavor—"so bad it's good"—of its unreality. That sublime clunkiness. The garish miscalculations with regard to makeup and line readings. The inexplicable gaps in visual continuity. The distancing effected by post-synchronized sound. The solemnly deployed papier-mâché props. The somnambulistic rigidity that afflicts every gesture. Those are what make it real and not just a movie. In a mere movie such things would be more artfully concealed.

How did you wander into this maze, anyway, and how would you get out? Do you in fact want to, or would you prefer to sink deeper into it, savoring its manifold ramifications and outlying distortions? You improvise, somewhat feebly because it is two in the morning and because by now you are feeling outnumbered by all these incorporeal projections, a little complaint to no one: "If only the spectator could speak. If only the spectator could become the projector and beam pictures out of his head. If the screen could become his dream. The producers tried to make it look like his dream, but it was obviously more practical to do it the other way around and make his dream look like their movies. They conspired to rewire the moviegoer's brain to conform with their specs, become a compatible receptor. 'Make 'em want. Make 'em remember. Make 'em want what they've been made to remember.' They set up a cheap pension plan for the imagination. Each spectator was guaranteed something to look back on, an alternate life. It may not be as tangible or intimate as you'd like, but it's always available and you can play it back endlessly.''

As a spectator you have to work hard to show you're alive and potentially ambulatory. You tend toward a condition of helplessness: immobilized, like Jimmy Stewart in a wheelchair in *Rear Window* or Olivia de Havilland trapped in an elevator in *Lady in a Cage;* unable to speak or cry out, like the mute Dorothy McGuire in *The Spiral Staircase;* straitjacketed in strips of linen like Boris Karloff when they buried him alive in *The Mummy,* incapable even of screaming as the mummy case was closed; strapped down, like the Frankenstein monster on the brink of being animated or the astronauts about to take off for the outer planets. Or merely as helpless as the infant locked into his high chair or swaddled in his Snugli, forced to gaze at whatever field of vision he is carried into.

If being a spectator has taught you anything it is how to be precisely the same spectator as the others—the Zero with a Thousand Faces—to ensure that *The Great Escape* can work the same on Times Square or near the headwaters of the Hudson or in a mercury-poisoned factory district of Lima. By responding appropriately and on signal, you participate in a great collective work, the binding together of the planet's inhabitants. If everybody tries hard we can all learn to laugh at the same failures of coordination, and lurch at the same throat-slittings.

How little of any of this you actually selected. A spectator can avoid certain movies, but not The Movies. You have been part of a captive audience all your life. Love it or leave it. But even if "they" permitted you to leave, there is no place to go. They own the airports. They own the telephones. They have seen to it that the pictures are everywhere. Swedish Hostage Syndrome begins to kick in. If you are to be strapped down and forced to watch these gigantic images, your survival odds improve drastically if you develop a fondness for them. Sharing a taste for movies with your captors will at least give you something to talk about.

You are nudged toward the conclusion that the movies have been provided for your benefit. The invisible producers— "They," the Atomic Rulers of the World—love you, all of you: your rods and cones, your pulse and neurons, every hyperreceptive inch of you. The way they explore your nervous system is an act of tenderness. They want you to be pleased. It would be terrible to think otherwise, just as it would be to think that you will not be given bread, or drinkable water.

And if the spectator—merely for the perverse satisfaction of imposing his will—wanted revenge? He could at best distort the playback, put the reels in the wrong order or mix different movies together. The last-ditch protest would be an angry collage. You would crouch over the dials, if you felt riled enough, and figure out a neat way to cross the signals. Confuse their beautiful story line, make a tape designed to drive everybody crazy instead of resolving the plot. You would sit up all night doing it, almost with enough concentration not to hear the bottles breaking against the wall of the discount outlet where they sell pirated cassettes of Spanish-Italian zombie movies.

Or try another way: return to the beginning of the spectacle, to the freshness and bewilderment of the first encounter. How can you get back? In a movie it would be sufficient to blur the image, overlay a harmonica honking out the "Memory" leitmotif, as the image turned to water and the secondary image (the slowly emerging picture of what was lost) broke through the shimmering surface. . . .

the garden of allah

First of all you'd have to write a biography of eyesight.

You'd have to lie awake in the dark, as if only by shutting the eyes off you could reexperience your induction into seeing. It would begin as an inventory of the places where you were before things had names: Float Town, Glareville, the Big Sheen, the Plain of Rustlings.

—But if they had no names, they weren't things, were they?

An infant eye waded in a space without a frame, slipping and sliding in and out of focus. Tumultuous roads spilled in random directions. The tight buds of paradise poked out of dogwood branches and an isolated halo of red neon announced Rick's Tavern. From somewhere inside the body you began to join up with a mosaic of gaudy pleasures: the weave of a bird's nest and the undulations of a Coke bottle, sunset seen through the window of Laraine Murphy's Shoreview Restaurant and the gaudy interior of Cinderella's coach seen through a Viewmaster stereoscope. The light-infested harbor quivered constantly with restless, coiling, galloping movements.

You roamed unmoored—a soft adaptable body—over the protrusions and crannies of the visible. Fissures interrupted the ground's facade, allowing glimpses of the hidden melodrama of nature. You stared into the secret storehouses— caves, basements, anthills, cocoons, hollow trees—as if they were the eyes of earth and air staring back. The roots and soil were unbounded, out of control. Look at any edge long enough and it broke apart. With its incoherent vegetative encroachment the wild field spoke a language inimical to human houses. The shrubbery unnamed you.

FOR ITS EDUCATION in focus and order the eye was indebted to certain privileged windows: objects whose function was to teach what an object was. They dropped down from nowhere like the black monolith in 2001. The world of the humans was dotted with other, miniaturized worlds: picture books, comic strips, kaleidoscopes, stereoscopic disks, log cabins on which snow fell, the Bazooka Joe cartoons wedged into packages of bubble gum, the flashing jungles and pirate ships of pinball machines, mannequins in department-store windows, fun-house apparitions, wax-museum monsters. These were rootless entities. Each had a platform set apart for it. Each was an invitation toward a center, as aggressive as a carnival barker: "Step right up and see the snake woman! See the mighty Hercules bending iron rods with his bare hands! Thrill to comets and exploding stars! Plus, for this exhibition only, authentic torture instruments of the dreaded Spanish Inquisition!"

But the invitation remained tantalizingly conditional. Each object stopped frustratingly at its edges. None was yet the authentic looking-glass world, where you would be able to pass through the mirror and move the furniture around and keep going deeper in. Not even the television screen, which promised so much and to which a whole room was consecrated, as if to certify it as the dwelling's newly established altar. But initially it took a certain amount of blind faith to find wonders in a machine that had not yet advanced beyond monochrome drabness. Through a sooty window you eavesdropped on people in cramped rooms. The habit could be acquired only by diligent practice.

The television did have noise, however. People *listened* to it, caught up as they still were in the culture of the ear. Radio had taught them how to respond to the studio orchestra calling for attention, the rumbling of cars and copters, the child crying over his wounded dog. The pictures were there to fill out the words a little. Noise was reassuring. Radio and television, like the refrigerator and the light above the kitchen sink, rattled and buzzed to show they were alive. The humming miracle of electricity erupted within its allotted corners, imparting a knowledge of hair cream, police stations, Teresa Brewer, airplane crashes, and Captain Video. It was as if the radio and the TV set *knew* what they were broadcasting, as if they contained a store of words just waiting to be enthusiastically ingested.

None of these devices could quite erase the home. Their limitation was to be crowded by furniture and ambient conversation. From time to time one family member or another fought to keep the volume loud enough to drown out everything else. A soundproofed room would have been required, within whose padded walls the music or the television program would be the only presence, with nothing to cramp its style.

A BOLDER ESCAPE was possible. You could pull up stakes and go to the movies, as you might take a transcontinental train ride or climb a mountain. The movie screen, in its imperial habitat on Market Street, was considerably more than a window. You had to pass through a number of intermediary zones—ticket booth, popcorn stand, usher's station—even to approach it. After passing through a region of silence and blindness the spectator slid into the seat and submitted to an unearthly visitation.

It took some getting used to—its purposes were not always clear—but without doubt this was the strongest medicine, the model for every other simulacrum. There might, in China or on Mars, be a more total sensory invasion, but for this time and place the movies were it. Simply by their existence they gave meaning to the otherwise obscure phrases with which the lobby was placarded, the long words which offered a preliminary hint of the gravity of adult language: mighty spectacle, epic magnificence, towering splendor.

The visual field was situated in the middle of the twentieth century. The infant spectators, however, were as yet unaware of having been born into a boundless screening room. They had still to learn that all the rooms—and the buildings that contained the rooms and the incorporated townships that contained the buildings—were subsidiary units within a networked multiscreen complex. The gardens were planted over buried circuitry. The sleeping quarters and lunch counters were conveniences, concession stands fitted in between projection sites. It would take much stumbling about in the world to determine that every location existed within a single Archive of Spectatorship.

The displays were scattered strategically: here a phosphorescent aquarium, there a diorama of an excavated city. The installation was so big it took years even to begin to map out a floor plan. The codes of instruction were themselves secreted in capricious corners, as if to simulate randomness. A copy of *TV Guide;* a pinup girl spray-painted on the side of a jet bomber; a Dick Powell number that someone's aunt remembered after a third round of Thanskgiving sherry; a plot summary of *Peyton Place* in a well-thumbed copy of *Photoplay* piled up at the barber shop along with *Police Gazette, Saga,* and *Popular Mechanics;* a guest on the Milton Berle show imitating Jimmy Durante; Heckle and Jeckle reenacting Marx Brothers patter; a caricature of Burt Lancaster confronting Alfred E. Neuman in the pages of *Mad;* a postcard of the pavement outside Grauman's Chinese Theatre. From such clues you could at least make preliminary notes toward the Visitor's Guide that no one had thought to issue.

The quest for the Key to Exhibits was rooted in love. Its source lay in the memory of an initial freshness in the relation between eye and screen. There had been an infatuation, born of the shock of immersion; and there was already, whether at nineteen months or four and a half years, a nostalgia for a vividness beginning to wear off. You had learned to identify things by looking at them again and again. By the time you knew for sure what they were, there was inevitably regret for the unrecoverable strangeness of a world without names.

ON THE BORDER between the named and the unnamable, between public screens and private houses, there was a phenomenon called "home movies." Grandmother stood in the yard. The projector hummed portentously, as if the noise made the pictures materialize. She stood motionless, dignified, her glance directed toward a row of early crocuses. The blurred focus made the trellis by which she was framed seem softer and therefore grander: a shape whose contours bled gently into the overcast air of early April. Then she shifted her head, looked directly into the camera, and smiled self-consciously. The shot was cut short. She disappeared.

But this was December, not April. Grandmother was not in the room. The garden was buried under snow. The watery luminous scene the family watched in the darkened living room was an uncanny retrieval. As if in the laboratory of Doctor Faustus, the dead blossoms quivered. The child at that moment discovered Eden. The yard in the movie was the same yard that stretched outside the window. But that was a yard that became mud or ice. The one on the screen remained in a permanent condition of early April. It blossomed at the family's bidding.

But how much of grandmother was in the frame? In some

sense it *was* her—an imprinting of her body on light-sensitive emulsion—but almost nothing of her was in the film, not her accent or her crossword puzzles or the rhythm of her days. You had to fill in what was missing. The movie was changing her into an abstraction. Of course, your knowledge of her was already limited—most of her life and thoughts would remain forever mysterious—but the movie limited that knowledge even more: because in time the movie did become her. The moment in the garden became a static pattern, a cutout divorced from life. To discover Eden was to discover in the same instant your estrangement from it.

That the process of showing movies was physical, controllable, and infinitely repeatable provided a definite sense of security: the strips of film wrapped around the reel, looped through the slot, guided by sprocket holes past the lightbeam. Dust glistened in the ray that bisected the room. The projector gave off a characteristic smell of heated metal which became the smell of resurrection, the odor of yards and bodies brought to life out of nothing. The odor of mere blur: the shoulder hurtling beyond camera range, the clump of red jacket blocking out light, the sloppily truncated grin, the unanticipated incursions of shadow and glare. The motion of the pictures was demonstrably organic by its jerkiness and chaos: an eerie alternate life form.

There was a nondescript handful of other 8-millimeter reels around the house, projected so often that the duration of each image became an intimately familiar geography. It was a sensual pleasure to anticipate precisely when, in the Sinbad cartoon, the island would rise out of the water or the roc's egg burst open. To appreciate the contour of a movement was something like falling in love with time. Part of the pleasure consisted in discovering that the movies did not merely move: the movements were *fixed,* permanently inscribed. To say for the first time ''I've seen this movie before'' was to know that each moment in the loop would come around again and again, forever.

You could learn to live in the preordained rhythms of that other life, embracing the fatality with which the lovers moved toward their dying fall or the necromancer readied the trap in which he himself would inevitably be snared.

And then there were a few silent and educational items, murky and thick-grained. Orphans were fed by missionaries in China. A little Mexican girl and her brother played outside an adobe hut while her mother prepared tamales. You felt that the Mexican children in the movie existed. They must be friends of the family, because your parents had movies of them, just as they did of aunts and grandparents and cousins. The children and their mother were part of the collection of things and words and activities that made it a family.

Where was all this happening, really? It was 1949 or 1951 or 1953. But you could not have known that yet. Even if you were acquainted with the numbers you couldn't yet guess what they measured. You had no idea what part of the world your house was in. The house was the world; the projected pictures of China and Mexico were its decor.

EACH CLAN HAD its own cache of images, its unique alphabet of birthday celebrations and summer holidays, its distinctive cast of elders waving from lawn chairs. But these reels did not provide a means of communication beyond the limits of the clan. The uninitiated could read nothing in the hieroglyphs with which the family communicated to itself.

It was at this point that the other class of movies—"real" movies—came into play. The outsiders who knew nothing of Aunt Patricia or Asbury Park were nevertheless intimately familiar with *King Kong, Mighty Joe Young, Gunga Din, The Lost Patrol*. These were a cultural currency permitting everyone to transcend the tribal, a modern global lingo penetrating the ethnic and professional enclaves of the families. It was the birth of cosmopolitanism.

The movies were such rare things to have, to see, to have captured. But what were they? Were those slippery light patterns "things" at all? They eluded you, always: they moved and kept moving. *Movie*. What a silly, infantile word it was. Baby's first sentence: "It movie, daddy." The flickering of the boxlike television was already a disturbance. A piece of furniture was supposed to sit still, not wave and beckon as if it insisted on being part of the room. Or perhaps it insisted on luring someone into it: those shifting bands of dots were really waves, and if you went too close you might get sucked into their undertow and drown in the same waters from which Lassie was at that moment rescuing a fallen child. The moving image could not be duplicated or controlled or played back. It could only be attended to, waited for.

Learning how to surrender to it was like learning to swim: coming to terms with the laws of a heavier and mysteriously pleasurable element. It was a river of images. You were not permitted to turn back, or to flip through it, or to look down on it from above. You could not determine in advance where it was leading. The surrender was ecstatic and terrifying.

And there was the further terror—as you came back in the dark after your first haunted-house picture—of being unable to control the return of the images. You had not sought the hell-mouth that gaped behind closed eyelids, the angry doctor smiling thinly as he tendered his scalpel, the flayed face of the melting beast: but now they belonged to you.

Everything had to be learned from scratch. The room in the image had other rooms in back of it. Occult pathways— streets, corridors, the past—led into it and away from it, in patterns as complex as the history of the world. It *was* the history of the world. Patiently you worked it out, crux by crux. Yet for most of childhood the continuity of the stories resisted decipherment.

It took so long to learn to recognize the faces of those people, and to understand what they were doing. Why did he allow his voice to deepen into a growl? Why did she let the hand mirror smash? How many hundreds of hours did you have to watch before having any real idea how the movie got from one scene to another, and what happened between? Most of the time you had no choice but to accept blindly what occurred. The shape of certain large events gradually came loose from the tumult of gestures and chatter: the wedding, the chase, the comical pratfall, the lovers' quarrel, the mad scene, the police investigation, the battle, the awards cere-mony.

TELEVISION HAD BEEN a rehearsal for movie theaters, just as eating at home was a rehearsal for restaurants. There was a solemnity in being allowed to go inside to view the real thing. What no one had prepared you for was the cascading chaos of it. You came in in the middle. You stumbled in the dark aisle because—from the moment you banged through the swinging door clutching a bag of M&M's—your eyes were fixed on the gigantic lumbering silhouettes of what proved to be frogmen cutting their way into enemy water. (You chewed, in the dark, as if it were the pictures you were swallowing.) After a while they appeared to be seized by agents in foreign uniforms.

You needed some kind of dictionary for the things on the screen, but there were too many of them and they changed all the time. What is a frogman? What is a uniform? What is an enemy? By then it was a different scene. You had no idea what was going on. Big faces wept or became angry. Some of the people wore helmets or dresses. What were they doing? Running up a flight of stairs. Tearfully crying out a name. Becoming inaudible in the noise of engines and bullets. Drowning in the bottom of a ship, fighting to reach a hatchway. And suddenly being somewhere else, being someone else—the one in a dress, in a space devoid of engines and bullets, writing a letter, or looking for a long time at a photograph. The picture of the photograph made the music get loud.

It was like eavesdropping on a language of which you grasped only every second or third word. There was a string of recognizable but unaccountable fragments. The evident purpose of the pictures and the music was to make people weep. The man and woman had wanted to embrace but they were prevented. They were made to say goodbye and move in opposite directions. Widening distance was the emblem of tragedy: the train went down the track, the boat became a speck.

The characters used up their emotional strength trying to make things come nearer. By force they wanted to change the bodies seen at a distance into faces seen close up. She was forced to fold towels bravely or stare in silent pain through rain-drenched windows. When the man in the helmet climbed into the airplane and it took off you had to tilt your back to watch it enter the sky, almost as if someone forced your head into the correct position. "Mommy, what is a Korea?"

Agonies were laid bare: a world of punishments, ambushes, disasters at sea. The soldier was condemned to march until he collapsed in the mud or was taken prisoner and or was court-martialed for collaborating with his Chinese captors. Cochise leaped from the top of a rock with a knife in his hand. The stockade burned. The one called Tony Curtis wept and confessed to the one called Frank Sinatra that he was an inadequate soldier. Joanne Woodward was compelled to change into sexy clothes and walk into a nightclub and lean against soldiers. Nuns tried to keep children from being killed by Germans. An escaped prisoner stumbled wounded along a dark cobbled street—glistening in the rain—and the music urged him to seek out the woman who waited on the other side of the barbed wire, the woman who would die with him or hold him cradled in her arms while he died.

And at night in your dream you were a frogman gliding under a hull, until you too were taken prisoner and thrust in front of a Japanese firing squad.

The hill you ran down was suffused henceforth with background music, as if in a truly real world everything would be underscored. In the silent yard, in the merely half-real open air, it took desperate attention to hear the violins almost breaking through.

The music was above all the sound of death. A bugle backed by string orchestra accompanied heroic final gasps. You died a thousand times: snowbound, trampled by stampeding cattle, crushed by falling towers, starving slowly in the midst of a hopeless retreat southward across the Inchon peninsula, devoured by leeches, crabs, alligators, army ants, mowed down from a Jap machine-gun nest upon hitting the beach at Tarawa, or standing upright and motionless after the showdown and then slowly and silently crumpling into the dust, like Burt Lancaster at the end of *Vera Cruz*. (The 1954 audience was fooled for half a beat into thinking he was still alive.)

A lonely cross poked up out of a makeshift grave in the wilderness: or a whole row of sabers in the Sahara to commemorate *The Lost Patrol*. "That man will never die." Death was that condition in which violin music soared to an intolerable pitch so that the hero could at last be safely buried—invisible but somehow persisting—within the bosom of the undying image.

THE KIDS IN the neighborhood had seen many movies by now, and had even learned almost all there was to know about endangered caravans, men half-mad with thirst, eyes peering through underbrush, alligators breaking the surfaces of rivers, lost explorers starting at the rumble of distant drums, burning arrows flying over the walls of stockades, cavalry troops riding into canyons.

Once the model had been established they could find movies everywhere. Only a slight variation in intensity distinguished the real movies on the screen from the numberless movielike artifacts and experiences: the expedition through the crazy house at the seashore park, the skeletons of dinosaurs rearing up in the natural history museum, the comic-book adventures of ghosts and ducks and Stone Age hunters, the episodes of drama or history isolated on bubble-gum cards, the three-dimensional plays staged with metal-and-rubber figurines, the movie stars proffering cigarettes or facial cream in the pages of *Look* and *The Saturday Evening Post,* the fragmentary violence of the drugstore book covers with their brawling mobsters and strangled blondes. In yard and playground and parking lot the children enacted poses copied from production stills.

Through the bush telegraph of the electric world the children got word of the movies that were coming. Some hadn't even been filmed yet. Some had opened in a far-off city and had not yet come to town, or might never come; and some they might in any event be forbidden to see. Advance messages arrived in comic-book versions, in paperbacks of the novels the movies were based on, in lobby posters glimpsed as they exited from the matinee showing of *The African Lion* or *The Lone Ranger and the Lost City of Gold.*

From the posters and the newspaper ads they learned many phrases: "Frank and revealing!" "Shattering power!" "The emotional experience of a lifetime!" "All the human depth and electrifying drama of the tremendous best-seller!" The concepts were still vague: they did not yet, for instance, know precisely what "human depth" meant. It suggested an intimate but still foreign space, a network of hallways inside an adult body.

They were haunted by the titles of all the movies they had missed. Each title stood for a story that might have been different from all the other stories, if only they could have experienced it. Each was a door, and there were thousands of doors they had not entered. They imagined themselves in the dark watching whatever such a title might denote, a place with different-colored vegetation, exotic legal codes, novel varieties of emotion and behavior. There was no telling how deep the space concealed by the name might be. Each was like a planet hidden under cloud cover.

It might be simply a name: *Rebecca* or *Diane*, *Hondo* or *Jubal*, *Moonfleet* or *Dragonwyck*. Was it the name of a woman, a house, a ship, a dynasty, a treasure, a crime? And why would any one name be so overwhelmingly powerful that a movie had be named after it?

It might be plainly in another language, a sound of imminent unknown danger: *Odongo*, *Jivaro*, *Mogambo*, *Simba*, *Huk!*, *Bwana Devil*, *Macumba Love*. It might simply specify the place where the strange erupted into the real—*Istanbul*, *Malaya*, *Tanganyika*, *Timbuktu*, *Beyond Mombasa*, *East of Sumatra*—or add some notation of the action that took place there: *Flight to Hong Kong*, *Flight to Tangier*, *Escape to Burma*, *Storm over the Nile*.

It might suggest a world of infinite choreographic frivolity, where adults wore bright clothes and laughed wildly, a drunkenly exuberant picnic: *You Can't Run Away from It*, *It Happens Every Spring*, *Everybody Does It*, *The More the Merrier*, *It Should Happen to You*, *It Happened to Jane*, *It Had to Happen*, *It Started with a Kiss*, *You're Never Too Young*, *It's Never Too Late*.

It might assume a riddling form. It referred to an event but provided no clues to its real nature. *The Man Who Died Twice.* How? *The Woman They Almost Lynched.* Why? *The Ship That Died of Shame.* Why? How? It spoke of fantastic and catastrophic events in the past tense, as if they had already occurred: *It Came from Outer Space, It Conquered the World, From Hell It Came, The Day the World Ended, The Day the Sky Exploded, The Night the World Exploded.* What? When?

It might, by contrast, conjure up an outpouring of vast cyclonic emotion, a potentially annihilating tumult urged on by violin ensembles: *All This and Heaven Too, All That Heaven Allows, Now and Forever, Goodbye Again, Never Say Goodbye, Heaven Can Wait, There's Always Tomorrow, Tomorrow Is Forever.* Time was to be overwhelmed by feeling. How would anyone make a photograph of that?

Those domains of large feeling were inhabited by companies of equally enormous humans, who could be defined only by broad sweeps of adjectives: *The Proud and Profane, The Bold and the Brave, The Tall Men, The Violent Men, The High and the Mighty.* What would such people look like? What kind of heightened language and monumental gestures would that race of giants use?

Emotion could be tuned to an even shriller, more ominous pitch: *Too Much, Too Soon, They Dare Not Love, To the Ends of the Earth, None Shall Escape, The Damned Don't Cry, No Way Out.* It was something that somebody might scrawl on a window or a wall in a moment of ultimate panic.

It sketched an emotional landscape of conflagration—*Fox-fire, Fire Down Below, Flame of the Islands*—or meteorological upheaval—*Written on the Wind, Blowing Wild, Wild Is the Wind, Storm Fear, Storm Warning*—or simply promised to strip the world bare: *Naked Alibi, Naked Earth, The Naked Edge, The Naked Dawn, The Naked Street, The Naked Hills, The Naked Jungle.*

It was a voice, perhaps, trying (against a background noise

of breaking glass, someone having just hurled a bottle at a mirror) to scream out a confession: *I'll Cry Tomorrow, I Died a Thousand Times, I Want to Live!*

A good title was something to be recited again and again, an empowering chant. The strongest evoked the worst that could befall and warded it off through the sheer power of their syllabic configuration—*Bad Day at Black Rock, Pickup on South Street, Stakeout on Dope Street*—or through an arcane sort of number magic: *Riot in Cell Block 11, Seven Men from Now, Five Against the House, Ten Seconds to Hell, One Minute to Zero.*

The most endlessly mysterious were those that packed into a single word a world of undefined possibilities—*Illicit, Notorious, Ruthless, Shockproof, Dangerous, Caught, Caged, Cornered, Branded, Desperate, Forbidden*—as if the fullness of a life could be represented by one undifferentiated sign.

Those children occasionally wondered—looking across at the marquee and noticing how it filled the street and put a label on it, how it turned the street into a frame around a name—what would be the right name for the movie to be made of their lives.

TO BE MADE into a movie was salvation, because the picture could not die: it was life itself. The saturated hues of Technicolor constituted all by themselves a tropical garden, a warm bath at the end of the mind. It required only swimming-pool logic to wade out into the sarongs and geometries of South Seas movies and Esther Williams vehicles, *Pagan Love Song* and *Pearl of the South Pacific,* the gaudy recurrent dance parties of heathens and pirates and jungle princesses.

There was another aspect to this extended game of dress-up: it was called history. In that enchanted world, John Wayne conquered Central Asia (while making eyes at Debra Paget), Jack Hawkins built the pyramids (while having troubles with Joan Collins), Gary Cooper spoke Seminole (while flirting somewhat coyly with Mari Aldon), and (in *Yankee Pasha*) the American adventurer (Jeff Chandler) seeking to rescue his fiancée (Rhonda Fleming) from Barbary pirates stumbled into a Vegas-style harem populated by the Miss Universe finalists of 1952 and presided over by Lee J. Cobb.

Across the screen's shimmering surface floated a circus of elements—gauze and feathers, chain mail and drawbridges, Arabs and Indians, forests, pools, fires—among which the eye moved like a swimmer. They appeared, they shifted, they reassembled in different shapes and colors. At every instant they gratified. An arcane vocabulary categorized varieties of pleasure: CinemaScope, Technicolor, Eastmancolor, Trucolor, Cinerama.

The cowboy movies in particular existed to give prominence to certain colors: blue sky, green fir, ocher rockface, a Crayola landscape. In *The Naked Spur* or *The Man from Laramie* the spectator's function was to appreciate the solidity of the landscape and the force and velocity with which the actors moved through it. Some ultimate reassurance about the thereness of things was implicit in the arroyos and salt flats of the desolate territories where grizzled old scouts—Arthur Hunnicutt, Walter Brennan, Millard Mitchell—cooked bacon and read sign. At the end the producers expressed their gratitude to Montana or Utah for existing. But where had there ever been such places outside of a movie?

Technicolor made scant distinction between the actual lakes

and mountains of the westerns and the man-made costumes and furnishings appropriate to *Knights of the Round Table* or *The Band Wagon.* It was all equally and ravishingly unreal. The lens converted even sky and sea into artificial constructions. The air was different in those bright outdoor scenes that could be observed only in a darkened interior: it was sustenance.

The deep hunger that it fed defined itself most vividly through trappings, frivolities, backdrops. Bric-a-brac was essence. The ribbons and packaging were busy enough in themselves that you barely needed to follow the plot or notice the new faces of 1957: Taina Elg, Diane Varsi, Miyoshi Umeki, Russ Tamblyn, John Gavin. The actors were there to provide a support system for the props and costumes, to give the camera something to encircle or swoop down on.

The screen was a second sky, where what you saw was nothing compared to the anticipation of what you might at any moment witness: a shooting star, a spaceship, an apocalypse. Going to the movies involved, always, a religious sense of hope. An incipient sense of worshipful attention was ready for the unimagined, the barely imaginable, God or world war or Martians. You wanted visible proof.

IN SUNDAY SCHOOL, reference was made repeatedly to certain uncanny and world-shaping events, but that was hearsay. Church amounted to little more than an anteroom to actual experience, a place where things were spoken of at a distance. Listening to Bible stories was at best like listening to tantalizing synopses of forthcoming releases. It wasn't quite enough, any more than leafing through back issues of *Photoplay*

was enough. The thirst was to *see* the truth, to be overwhelmed by it.

That was what movie theaters were for: they were the
places where something real was going on, where plagues and
floods really happened. A verbal account of the Red Sea parting or the Angel of Death gliding over the rooftops of Egypt
couldn't compare to witnessing it in *The Ten Commandments*. It
couldn't even compare to the trailer for *The Ten Commandments*. Why settle for words when you could go see photographs of God? And if He couldn't quite (considering the
buildup) measure up—if the burning bush was, after all, not
sufficiently different from the brushfires of *Flaming Feather* and
The Flame and the Arrow and *Fire over Africa,* and if (to one's
secret disappointment) they didn't even *show* God—that was
surely not the fault of the movies.

God was not interesting if He only occurred in the remote
past and was incapable of being played by a movie star. If the
most important thing in the world was invisible, how important could it be? It was fitting that there *should* be a movie of
God, a movie that would live up to what the promotional kit
for *The Big Fisherman* promised: "the stirring physical action,
the massive spectacle, and the exalted spiritual theme." He
belonged in that atmosphere, and would ultimately be judged
by its standards, in the same way it was said of certain famous
stage actors that they just couldn't make it in the movies.

It was when your world blacked out and the other radiant
world imposed itself that you understood the word "awe."
The kingdom of heaven consisted of robed Saracens, half-
naked princesses, ululating high priests, dust-covered troupes
of elephants and camels, earthquakes and cobras, thousands of

bits of metal clanking in unison, an ensemble sustained by the rumbling of a gigantic orchestra. It was the authentic noise and texture of an ancient alien planet.

Wasn't this like the effect of prayer, to have such things realized? To be enabled to see those hosts of armed warriors assembled? To travel those enormous distances—soaring into the air and crossing over plains and mountains—and in the midst of it to hear the voice of God in all its thunderous sonority? The voice alone would not have meant so much. The manifold glory lay not in the voice but in the thousands of extras and horses and terraced palaces assembled at its command.

Whereas the empty church was just empty. You and your friends crept in one afternoon as if expecting to find God relaxing at home. There was nothing. That is, there was nothing *playing* there. Some awkward posters of Jesus at table, by a lake, on a hill, patting children on the head, smiling at lepers: coming attractions. But those illustrations were drained images, not remotely as gritty or turbulent as the lobby cards for *Demetrius and the Gladiators* or *The Big Fisherman*. If God was anywhere He was across town working wide-screen miracles.

NOT THAT ALL the movies had His stamp on them. It was a gradual education to scout the borders of the diabolical territories in which scenes, subplots, and whole movies might be located. There was a curse on some movies, so that you could never undo the fact of having seen them. The loop would run again and again. You enter the steamy little movie theater in the tropical port and find a movie about a steamy little tropical port. The white men, in white jackets, penetrate a clearing. They have to bend their heads to get into the hut. There is a fire on the screen. Voodoo drums. Piles of skulls. An amulet made of twisted roots. The dancers move in a circle. The eyes move toward the center of the screen where the center of the ritual is happening. Ceremonial cooch dance.

Americans break a taboo and are cursed. Having violated the sanctuary of the cobra goddess, they will each be seduced in turn by the beautiful woman (Faith Domergue) who deep down is cobra. The bedroom scenes elide into slithers and hisses. "You ready for me, baby?" Scream and darkness. It's never what is shown, it's what is about to be shown: the threatening music, the camera inching toward the unspeakable. But in the end you remember best the act of entering the theater, as if the theater were itself the forbidden tropical clearing given over to the power of cobras and skulls and amulets.

It was the source of the talk. You talked your way out of what the images had made you feel. Limit their power by tagging them—or get rid of the curse by passing it on to someone else. For every frightening and forbidden image you had seen, there were thousands more of which you had only heard. A daily seminar filled in the blanks. From the beginning movies were incorporated indissolubly into a system of orally transmitted folklore.

Older brothers came home late from the movies and could be overheard talking on the phone, or sitting up late in the kitchen telling what happened in the last reel of *Try and Get Me*—how the lynch mob set the jail on fire, how the terror was visible on the face of the trapped kidnapper as they lifted him from his cell and passed him like a doll over the heads of the crowd—or how Gene Krupa was a junkie—or how Kim Novak saw a black-robed nun emerge from the darkness and was so surprised she fell backward off the belltower to her death—or how the aliens in *The Mysterians* abducted earth women to mate with them and repopulate their dying planet.

Retelling a movie was an art in itself. Children grew up telling each other plots. There would be sessions where the most frightening or disgusting episodes would be elicited from a circle of people. "The sickest thing I ever saw was when the giant ants invaded the communications room on board the ship in *Them!* and wrapped their pincers around the sailors' bodies." "The worst thing was the mark the aliens made on people's necks in *Invaders from Mars*." "They staked him out in the desert and coated him with honey and let the ants devour him." "The mask had nails inside it." "The man sent her a pair of binoculars that poked her eyes out." You didn't have to have seen it, hearing about it was bad enough. Years were spent trying to define the precise point where pleasure became disturbance, the border between too upsetting and not upsetting enough.

The folklore had to do with aliens in sunglasses who drank blood and whose language had to be translated by subtitles, baby monsters spawned by radiation, husbands who devised clever methods of murdering their wives or driving them insane and detectives who laid equally clever traps to catch them, exotic tortures practiced by Apaches and medieval warlords, children abducted by desert marauders, bombing raids in the big war against Germany and Japan and Russia and Korea, madmen whose urge to kill was unleashed by particular melodies or colors, people haunted by dreams that told them they had lived another life before this one, archaic chants that brought mummies to life. Stories of miracles, all of them, like Lazarus clambering groggily from his tomb in the stiffly un-coordinated manner of a resurrected Boris Karloff.

The real miracle was simply that those creatures lived and moved. Once set in motion, the legions of walking ghosts never stopped. The thousands of celluloid beings who inhab-ited movies were like windup toys that would run for eternity, or like the proliferating animate mops unwittingly activated by the sorcerer's apprentice in *Fantasia,* or like the irradiated insects who in *Them!* and *Tarantula* and *The Deadly Mantis* seemed on the verge of sweeping over the earth's surface. At night, in the dark, the disembodied creatures swarmed in the mind, indestructible.

a short history of fun

As a medium in which the dead continued to walk about, movies provided an education in time. You had been watching a multiscreen documentary on the aging process. Events could be dated by which actors were still alive, or by how many wrinkles they had acquired. The unnatural difference here was that the process could be reversed, the past restored. The cinematic Shangri-La where Ronald Colman and Jane Wyatt stayed forever young really did exist: it was the movie itself, preserving them intact and luminous.

But when you exited from *Lost Horizon* the world hit you in all its sunlit rotting physicality: a shock depicted in aggravated form in the film's last reel, when Margo shriveled up the minute she transgressed beyond the territorial limits of

Shangri-La. Movies made the way real people got old—in linear order, and more or less at the same rate—seem clunkily old-fashioned. They made time itself old-fashioned, the regular sort where a second was always precisely a second, and where each second trooped dutifully behind the last. Movies could speed it up, slow it down, reverse it, make it stand dead still.

You new children enjoyed, without remotely realizing it, a privilege none of your ancestors could savor: to look at the movies your parents watched, the movies your grandparents watched, and by that secretive gaze to appropriate the childhoods of the people who gave birth to you. You could even try (and it was one of the more delicate educational exercises the world afforded you) to grasp the muted sorrow of the grownups at seeing Gable and Garbo young, and Leslie Howard and Carole Lombard alive.

It was at first disturbing to learn that there were dead movie actors. (This was often how it slipped out that death existed.) At mid-century most were still alive. Night after night they showed up on *The Stork Club* and *The Colgate Comedy Hour,* doing soft-shoe numbers and evoking incomprehensible peals of laughter with trademark grins and pauses, tirelessly reiterating an unalterable persona: the Miser, the Egotist, the Drunkard. They were as peculiar as uncles, and eventually as familiar: Uncle Jack, Uncle Jimmy, Uncle George, Uncle Bing. It took years for their tics to become lovable. At first they functioned more neutrally, as shoal markers that made possible an intimate navigation through the world. By default a bond came to exist. A person whose name and face were identifiable was not a stranger, not one of the unknowns who filled the plazas and terminals of downtown.

The family helped with the introductions. It was necessary
to explain about radio and vaudeville and the rest of the warm,
dense world the performers came from. ''It was cold in those
days. There was no money, no television. In between wars
there were Kay Kyser and Fred Allen and the Andrews Sisters.'' The performers in turn introduced other performers,
young ones who had been given a chance to costar in *Ten North
Frederick* or *Paris Holiday*. The family was constantly inducting
new members: for the constellation of performers was, if not
truly a family, at least an extension of the system of which the
family was the crux.

The system bound people together by linking names to
faces. When you were becoming a member of a family, the
primary task was to get everybody's name straight. It had
taken years to learn the names of all the relatives, and to figure
out the relationships through which they earned their seat at
the annual feasts. Now there were these other names, hundreds of them, ancient (Roscoe Karns, May Boland, the Ritz
Brothers) and modern (Dorothy Malone, Cameron Mitchell,
Pier Angeli). And they themselves had relationships: Joan Fontaine was Olivia de Havilland's sister and Marisa Pavan was
Pier Angeli's sister, George Sanders was Tom Conway's
brother and Scott Brady was Lawrence Tierney's brother! But
somehow they were not so difficult to disentangle as the family. Their function was more obvious: they appeared in movies. Jeff Chandler's identity consisted solely of having starred
in *Broken Arrow, Foxfire,* and *Sign of the Pagan*. His existence
needed no further explanation or justification.

That they were benevolent would have been clear even if
they had not constantly embraced on television, amiably rib-
bing one another about their parsimony or the shape of their

nose. They lived to please, to make themselves available. They *agreed* to play parts, so that everyone could have a little piece of them: they turned themselves into common property. They made it possible to share perceptions, to talk about the weather of the world: "Isn't that Mitzi Gaynor?" "Wasn't she in *The Birds and the Bees*?" "Was that the one with David Niven?" "Wasn't he wonderful in *The Moon Is Blue*?" "I love that man, I really do, I adore his accent." Their names became an indispensable component of language, a vocabulary of essences consisting of people rather than ideas.

THAT THE ACTORS were human made the world they came from—the world of old movies—alluring in a way that no library or museum could ever be. Those weren't engravings or statues back there, those were *people*. They were alive, they smiled at you from a distance. You were grateful for the happiness they afforded, and could hardly resist going back for more. It was easy to override a tiny nagging reluctance, an internal warning that the beautiful lost world was somehow a forbidden zone. To move backward in time, no matter how often you did it, induced a constant low-level jet lag to which you simply had to accustom yourself.

Time travel represented the wall that technology was unable to breach. The modern-age machines that could speed up time and cut through space—radio and electric hair dryers and atom bombs and jet planes—still could not take you even one second backward into what had been. Just how badly people wanted to move in reverse could be gauged from their chosen environment, a gallery of animated replications. You could at least send your eyes and ears, if not your body, back in time.

You had only to pretend that the moving pictures were real to have an eerily facile access to vanished universes. World War II was still playing on every other channel; on the Four O'Clock Feature, week after week, Glenn Miller invented jazz. Having once adjusted to that immobilized but alert half-life, you could spend much of your time comfortably eavesdropping on the past, mastering its lingo and popular songs and dance steps, imprinting your brain with the hairstyles and lighting effects of a time before your birth. You could learn all the stories, become acquainted with all the power figures: Dr. Caligari, Dracula, King Kong, Little Caesar, George M. Cohan.

To absorb all that information was like living several different lives. In further pursuit of such knowledge you would eventually enter museums, archives, unfurnished screening rooms in Manhattan office buildings where old men gathered to pay homage to Leatrice Joy or Blanche Sweet, tiny theaters where 16-millimeter prints of *Un Chien Andalou* or *The Blood of a Poet* were put on display, or tune in to Channel Eleven in the middle of the night because a rare 1936 aviation movie was showing. The century had been placed under electronic surveillance, and your self-appointed task was to monitor the tapes.

IN SO DOING you were only one agent of an army that apparently included just about everybody. Unbeknownst to one another you had each been inducted into the secret world society of watchers. People got to a point where they felt they had been stationed outside history, watching the decades unreel, each with its special subjects, its unaccountable predilections. The decades were not successive but simultaneous. Philo Vance continued to proffer his cigarette case with self-satisfied elegance as if unaware that it was no longer 1932. Certain individuals developed specialized tastes for particular years: there were self-created 1929 people, 1957 people. "I've been in the forties for months." History was the rack from which they picked hats and gloves, witticisms and court-ships.

Hardly anything was allowed to go away. Nor was that merely for purposes of daydream: each image had its potential uses. No telling which might have unexpected resale value. An excavated Myrna Loy vehicle might offer ideas for furniture, ideas for hairstylings, useful gag lines and period slang. Maybe you could pick up an old song overdue for revival, mine plot material for a television script. The future was going to be crammed with the past. Somebody told you that hologram simulations of all the movie stars who ever lived were being readied for possible deployment as a zombie force of laser-generated simulacra.

You could end up adopting a whole life. Young people chose to become dead actors, walking around in borrowed accents and clothes. James Dean went everywhere. Newly prosperous coke dealers studied Cary Grant's timing hoping something would rub off. The girl in the bar transformed herself into Marilyn Monroe and the whole place went crazy with her slit skirt and blondness and line readings.

It could get out of hand; there was such a thing as caring too much. Some found it necessary to follow Jimmy into his death car, to share Marilyn's pills. Ten thousand maniacs studied photographs of actors, like Dana Andrews beginning to lose himself in Gene Tierney's portrait in *Laura*. In that spirit

Hinckley would end up shooting Reagan for Jodie Foster. The movies had taught people how to fall in love, and they returned the favor by falling in love with movies, with the faces in movies.

When Georges Demeny (in his 1892 article "The Talking Photographs") anticipated how happy people would be "if they could only see once again the features of someone now dead" and looked forward to "the replacement of motionless photographs, frozen in their frames, with animated portraits that can be brought to life at the turn of a handle," he meant that people would want to contemplate the simulacra of their relatives and loved ones. He could hardly have foreseen that they would choose instead to resurrect Maria Montez or Elvis Presley.

The sort of love felt by hard-core fans was dangerous. The compassion they lavished on their decaying idols could turn in an instant into the rage of the rejected and dispossessed. The room was to be kept exactly as it was the day she died, the lockets and heirlooms and framed photographs wiped free of dust on a daily basis (like Lana Turner's shrine to her alcoholic movie-star father in *The Bad and the Beautiful*), the drapes and windows opened and closed at various complicated intervals precisely as she, in her adorably imperious manner, would have insisted. A perfume was forced to linger well beyond its natural span, a memento preserved as carefully as Anthony Perkins's mother in *Psycho*.

EVERY MORNING THE movie lovers woke up wishing today was the day they were going by train to California to be a movie star, like Marion Davies in *Going Hollywood* or Carole

Lombard in *Twentieth Century,* in 1933 or 1934. It was a metaphor for being alive and in motion, surrounded by chaotic
swarms of humorous butlers, fast-talking agents and reporters,
and overburdened cops throwing up their hands in frustration.
Noise and lights, the dizzy clarity of the real. How they longed
to have been inhabitants of *that* century. And indeed they
were, for as long as the movie lasted.

They returned again and again to *The Awful Truth* or *To Have
and Have Not,* as to a place where they could be at peace. It
wasn't narrative that drew them but the spaces that the narrative permitted to exist: the mere doors, roadsters, parlors,
harbors. And beyond that, rarest of all, the infinitesimal rests
and silences that let them sit on the settee or bar stool and
breathe for a stolen second the air of the place.

By the mid-seventies it was almost possible to inhabit a
twenty-four-hour ambience of recycled Hollywood, modular
chunks of Busby Berkeley and Humphrey Bogart and Louise
Brooks recombined into lofts and discotheques and hair salons.
A culture of scavengers combed through a Salvation Army
store full of castaway film props and costumes, to retrieve an
Art Deco Bakelite ashtray or an intact fedora. Like the refu-
gees and paupers who in the Dark Ages slept in the ruins of
ancient Roman monuments, the dispossessed made a world
from fragments of Warner Brothers and Twentieth Century–
Fox: a girl wore a moth-eaten feather boa that belonged to her
imaginary grandmother Constance Bennett, her boyfriend the
smoking jacket of Ricardo Cortez. Soundtrack courtesy of Paul
Whiteman, Ruth Etting, and the Yacht Club Boys. Cinematography by champagne, cocaine, or Thai stick.

The thirties represented the richest of treasures, a wonder-

land of American speech, waitresses and taxi drivers, off-duty
night nurses comparing their silk lingerie, Joan Blondell, *Gold
Diggers of 1933, Stage Door.* It was enough to instill something
like patriotic pride, except that it went beyond America: a
universal urban language of glitzy impoverishment so over-
powering that it had to be simultaneously translated into *Osaka
Elegy* and *La Chienne* and *La Signora di Tutti,* to prove that all the
cities on the planet could be identified by the same elevated
trains, shop lights, and gramophones singing about the hope-
lessness of small-time romance.

In thirties plot lines there was a casual fatalism you could
live with, a no-nonsense rhythm that enabled you to be tragic
and chew gum at the same time: crooked politicians, unwed
mothers condemned to prison farms, comical organ grinders
and double-talking barflies, amnesia and manslaughter, ten
years of false imprisonment, sleuths with a knowledge of pedi-
greed dogs and Chinese vases, rich men's neurasthenic wives
making eyes at good-natured but not quite bright young truck-
ers, irascible fathers slamming doors and tripping over roller
skates, holdups, hurricanes, typhus epidemics, crooners keen
to make good in radio, tap-dancing scam artists topping each
other's one-liners, party girls finding God in rural backwaters,
irresponsible young artists crippled in drunken collisions. A lifetime in seventy minutes. A dream punctuated by dissolves and
montages: neon signs, calendar pages flipping, snowdrifts
and blossoms, champagne bottles popping amid noisemakers
and party hats. They brought you right into it, spun you
around, and then hauled you out as if nothing whatever had
happened.

More years went by than you cared to count. It had been

like wandering through the rooms of an almost infinitely large warehouse, constructed in Hollywood in the thirties and forties: an interior filled with custom-designed furniture and clothes and story lines. There all narratives slotted into each other, populated by a single family of stars and starlets and character actors as familiar as aunts and uncles. Dear old Hugh Herbert and Guy Kibbee and Edna May Oliver. It didn't matter if deep down you found them boring or even repulsive, they were kin. You knew them, therefore they were not frightening.

In living with them it became possible to imagine the time they had emerged from, a culture in which posters, magazines, and songs prepared the ground for each new attraction. The country of movies hummed with a constant unobtrusive bustle like the preparation for prom night or the county fair, adjustment of spotlights and microphones, hammering together of sets. At several decades' remove you found it possible to share the excitement of this constant reassuring ballyhoo. "What world are you in? You're in the world where *The Foxes of Harrow* is coming to this theater next week!"

The process by which the producers took care of their audience had had an almost democratic flavor. There had been a crying demand for a particular pairing of actor and actress. People needed for there to be a movie of *Dragonwyck* or *All This and Heaven Too*. To make a movie out of something was to make it available as an experience that could be effortlessly inhaled. The catch was that you couldn't do it by yourself. "They" had to do it for you; you hoped they would, wrote letters to the studio pleading with them to supply you with that experience. You could hardly wait to see how they would do it, who would play the parts. . . .

But after all (you realized as the watery shimmer and the theremin's "memory motif" hoisted you back through time again), that decision had been made in somebody else's life. The issue was closed. A movie was a completed destiny. It was hard at times to remember that you were not the intended audience for what you were watching. You were an accidental intruder, a spy from the future watching an ancient trap snap shut.

As the thirties wore on—that is, the imaginary thirties invented by the sixties and seventies—a haunting flavor of catastrophe insinuated itself even into football musicals and Arabian fantasies. Safe in the nostalgic future you monitored the early-warning signs of the disaster, as Nazi spies penetrated the desert kingdom of Ali Baba, and the cadets and midshipmen who had hitherto spent their time worrying about the big game or a date with their roommate's sister were adjusting to the possibility of sudden death.

Crudely interpolated elements of propaganda communicated the tremor of distant massacres. This incursion had the curious and oddly bracing effect of authenticating the movies. The lies were genuine wartime lies, forcibly wedged into place. Something was tearing things apart outside, something so unavoidable that gashes began to appear in the walls of the dream. An advanced exercise in extrapolation might even deduce, from analysis of the messages secreted in *Gung Ho!* and *Wake Island* and *Action in the North Atlantic,* precisely what unseen pressures had been brought to bear. The onscreen action had been *squeezed* into those configurations. The actors spoke under pressure, like prisoners of war.

The stressed fantasies of *Air Force* or *Objective, Burma!* set heroic adventurers moving with invulnerable flexibility through a dream landscape of fires and concealed assassins. In jungles and on beachheads the GIs traded cigarettes and baseball stats, carrying the relaxed cadences of small-town parks and Broadway saloons into alien territory. The enemy was a mute impersonal killing machine. The Americans, on the other hand, went to war leaping and grinning and joking. But for all their air of camaraderie, each was ultimately solitary, disconnected, saved by freedom of movement. They ad-libbed with anarchic grace, putting jeeps together out of spare parts (the Americans were mechanical whizzes) and inventing their tactics as they went along, while the humorless aliens tripped up on their perverted notions of obedience and unity.

The vigorous young actors who filled those roles had to mime death and amputation, on the same screen where the newsreel had just provided glimpses of actual combat. The imagination of the audience spliced the disparate images together, placing the actor who pretended to be dying against the backdrop of genuine tank attacks and naval battles. To set one image clashing against another was the most any movie could do. Frank Capra's *War Comes to America* pitted scenes of Fascist rallies, Nazi blitzkrieg, Japanese atrocities in China against home movies of American farms and schoolyards. The resulting visual field was a collage encompassing the known world. The gap between foreign violence and peaceful wheatfields was the breach through which invasion threatened.

The actor moved across the seam—as the audience, rapt and paralyzed, could not—and entered the intrusive newsreel footage. Once inside, by performing the gestures of a hero, he obliterated the offending images. *Back to Bataan* erased Bataan.

There was also a space beyond the reach of the war, a

heaven where lives were weighed and resurrections stage-managed. This was the last time—in *Stairway to Heaven* or *It's a Wonderful Life* or *Here Comes Mr. Jordan* or *A Guy Named Joe*—that anyone would try to explain the difference between life and death in a child's terms. In *The Ghost and Mrs. Muir,* the discontents of time and mortality dissolved into a stirring montage of waves breaking over rocks, set to spectral sonorities devised by Bernard Herrmann. It was the end of religion, and the filmmakers must have almost known it as they crafted their humorous afterlives, their bumbling or bureaucratic angels. They designed a soft death for the children to enter without terror, a welcoming and interminable Oz.

And there was a space beyond even the oversight of heaven. (It was wonderful the way the flat screen could be made to disgorge, infinitely, interiors within interiors. Forties movies excavated these hidden spaces because they needed them, needed hiding places even within their hiding places.) A soft-focus feminine Otherland was defined by cunningly interwoven dream sequences and flashbacks, by hypnotic voice-overs and spiraling camera movements, by aestheticized reenactments of childhood cruelties and whirlwind romances with quietly menacing strangers.

The male action picture had no past and no regrets; it slammed by and left nothing in its wake. The woman's picture was a dance of beauty and death, sacred to the memory of memory. Within its mirrored interiors—as if in compensation for the savage Holy War of combat movies—evil was allowed its subtleties and attractions. The sinister and the erotic flowed together. The sinuous, decorative microworlds of *Rebecca* and *Jane Eyre* and *Laura* and *Secret Beyond the Door* and *Letter from an*

Unknown Woman and *Portrait of Jennie* were full of corridors extending endlessly inward, memories from beyond the grave, a name repeated over and over for a lifetime, an obsessive recurrent glance on which all existence hung as on an invisible, unbearably taut string.

It was a thick and fluid dimension. The bodies floated out of carriages and up winding staircases, as if the music of Miklos Rozsa and Max Steiner were part of the air they breathed. This universe had always existed (in *Queen Christina*, in *Mayerling*), but now it came into its own territory: a dark flower glistening in the shadow of war. It was perhaps a muted warning: that these seductively enveloping interior spaces were what had been nurtured within the defense perimeter. Home became strange. A brief but telling cycle revolved around glamorous female murderers: *Ivy, Leave Her to Heaven, A Woman's Vengeance*.

Then—after the war—people could circle warily around each other in a world of nightclubs and truck stops, a backlit theater of memory where women's faces disappeared in cigarette smoke and the world was erased by the blare of rumba bands. All men were named Steve and hadn't shaved in three days, had been wounded in battle or betrayed in the bedroom, stopped off for coffee but couldn't get that tune out of their heads, had been out of work since they got back from the war, took no satisfaction in anything but a grim worn-out lucidity of purpose. The women were isolated, cynical, haunting, ruthless, frightened, doomed. Their intentions were crucial but definitively illegible. The rest of the world—cops, soda jerks, small-time hoods and con artists, rubes on the town flashing their wads, hat-check girls dreaming of movie careers, cunning drunkards, eccentric night clerks—didn't care anyway. The el rumbled by, indifferent to the lovers dying in its shadow.

Between the rain and the fog and the neon, and the theremin wails mimicking the inside of somebody's sick mind, there was the ordinary music of the dialogue, a free-floating vernacular symphony that made sense of the world one gag line at a time. A crook's moll, alluding to the clutter of perfume bottles on her dressing table: "I like to stink myself up." A small-time gangster asserting himself in the face of imminent catastrophe: "I'm no soda jerker! I'm not one of these broken-backed dummies that come into your soda store!" Another moll, asked where she's heading: "As far as twenty bucks and a mink coat'll take me."

As the forties turned into the fifties the smoke thinned out, the dense shadows got flatter and the camera setups more rigidly boxlike, the brilliant slang and juicy poeticism gave way to a more rudimentary Basic English ("Sergeant! Come here!"), the war vets and private eyes became cops and federal agents, the racketeers metamorphosed at times into Red agents, and the femmes fatales in the center of the frame withdrew, diminished, to its margins. Suddenly it was 1958, and the haunting movie of your dreams had become a television show, *Dragnet* or *M Squad* or *77 Sunset Strip,* its central characters reduced to third-generation photocopies of the original mythic presences.

THE FIFTIES PUT labels on issues: Korea. Psychoanalysis. Jet bombers. Communists. Juvenile delinquents. "Sometimes I think the only solution is to clear out all the people and drop an atom bomb on that whole slum.'' Split personalities. Psychopaths who kill because they read too many comic books. Jazz musicians cast adrift among drugs and gangsters. Public personalities with drinking problems. Marriage in the suburbs as an opportunity for bravura acting. Battle fatigue. Career paths: the white-collar warfare of *Executive Suite* and *The Man in the Gray Flannel Suit*. Love affairs, or the threat of them, between gardeners and suburban widows, restless veterans and repressed schoolteachers, teenage handymen and rich men's daughters, violently disaffected gang members and awkward honor students. Way at the end of the decade: panties (*Anatomy of a Murder*) and nuclear holocaust (*On the Beach*). As an abbreviation for all that was so ineffably shapeless and indigestible in the fifties, the trailer for M-G-M's *The Cobweb* promised: ''At last! The novel that bares the secrets of the psychiatrist's couch is now on the screen!''

On all sides heroes were overwhelmed by psychology, alcohol, narcotics, sexual trauma: boxers turned into drug addicts (*Monkey on My Back*), singers (*I'll Cry Tomorrow*) and comedians (*The Joker Is Wild*) got lost in drink, movie actresses coped with their father fixation by becoming nymphomaniacs (*Too Much, Too Soon*), baseball players coped with their father fixation by retreating into psychosis (*Fear Strikes Out*), mousy housewives found it necessary to diversify into a multiplicity of personalities (*The Three Faces of Eve*).

It was as if the fifties had been compelled to execute a tortuous slow-motion exposure of words and deeds and bodies, all snap and timing lost, every blow landing a bit more heavily than intended. A ponderous heaving and flailing approximated passion. In the midst of the wide-screen carnival arose grotesque parodies of the body: Jayne Mansfield, whose figure cracked men's eyeglasses and made milk boil over, and Jerry Lewis, a demon of hyperactive self-abasement sprung from some terminally inarticulate and uncoordinated netherworld. In them the body became loud. The movies in which they appeared—like the primary-colored sets that framed their gags—seemed to collapse around them.

The body was not the same size as the world. It was a bad fit, whether too big or not big enough: *Attack of the Fifty-Foot Woman, The Amazing Colossal Man, War of the Colossal Beast, Attack of the Puppet People, The Incredible Shrinking Man.* The appliances no longer worked right if your hands didn't match up with the handles. A change in physical dimensions was enough to turn ordinary behavior and emotions grotesque.

Jerry Lewis and Jayne Mansfield and the colossus and the shrinking man announced the new noise, the culture of the bad beginning to define itself through movies about deranged and violent teenagers or mutant insects. The grammar was brute contrast, the subject was violent disjuncture. A mess (a blob, an extraterrestrial eyeball, a bloodsucking Martian) broke into the world through a crack in the sky, the same way that hoodlums got into a candy store by smashing the window.

Grossly unlike elements coexisted in the new condition. People were forced to communicate by shouting or using sign language as brusque and rudimentary as the narratives within which they functioned: a federal agent disguised as a teenage drug dealer (*High School Confidential*), a space alien disguised as an American husband (*I Married a Monster from Outer Space*), surviving Nazis manipulating the religious customs of South Sea islanders (*She Demons*), or a rock-and-roll slumber party interrupted by a lesbian vampire (*Blood of Dracula*). Inadequate acting—whether rigidly inexpressive or coarsely excessive—

functioned as a tool to rip apart the upholstered elegance of the old movies. Few would have imagined at the time that these rough and obvious scrawls—as beyond interpretation as they were devoid of concealment—were precisely the texts for which succeeding generations would feel compelled to provide a gloss. They would look at them again and again, as if to trace a line of fracture.

A PROCESS OF accelerated obsolescence was at work, egged on by the energies of youthful barbarism. More immediate forms of gratification were required than the tortuous gyres of traditional plotting. Every instant of screen time had to be the climax. The street carnival of the sixties escalated the speedup, as moviemakers struggled to to keep pace with attention spans informed by strobe lights and sudden jolts of chemical inspiration. Spectators had for so long been able to second-guess what would happen on the screen that they needed some swift jolts to stay focused on the show. What they got, and relished, was a pandemonium of hip zaps, quick changes, and unexpected punch lines: "Fake-out!" Almost anything was okay, as long as it changed fast enough.

The pop aesthetic supplied everything but the incense: a paradise of legs (female), colors (glow-in-the-dark), raw chunks of actual street to prove it wasn't a movie, and the collage of rapid panning and cutting and zooming and angular compositions now openly recognized as "style." Newly synthesized textures, an optical equivalent of the miracle fabrics of previous decades: blurs, whirls, rainbows, jazzy silhouettes, composites. Solarized portraits like the photographs in fashion magazines whose purpose was not to depict their sitters but to transform them: Mick Jagger as open flame, John Lennon as psychotropic mushroom surrounded by fanciful artifical foliage, Bob Dylan as imprisoned blues singer bearing prophetic tablets. Complexity is sexy, silliness is complex, continuity exists to be disrupted. Nudity, motorcycles, hallucinations, Nixon jokes. Ronald Reagan and Victor Mature making guest appearances in the Monkees movie. Crude zoom shot equals the shock of the real. Third World revolution—*The Battle of Algiers, Burn!, Che!*—preferably with a soundtrack by Ennio Morricone.

With satisfaction the young audience watched the frontiers of nudity and language dissolve. Europe led the way, with contingents of erotically dissatisfied Swedish students and Danish housewives. Film by film the desiccated old laws dropped off. The empty space remaining was called freedom. The ground was being cleared for the New Eden, a voyeurist paradise in which there was nothing that could not be looked at. In strikingly different ways Roger Vadim and Federico Fellini began to sketch in the details of the new covenant, and a small army of film students, old-time exploitation experts, and consortiums of Western European businessmen followed their lead. The eye was to be fed. Desire was in the cameraman's seat. An age of optical luxury opened. The lens prepared to move into what had been curtailed by the fade-outs of the first half-century of movies, like conquistadors in silk paisley shirts embarking for an undiscovered continent.

IN SHORT ORDER the situation got so complicated that new explanations were needed, and then further ones to explain the explanations. Movies became visual handbooks for the new politics of provocation and conspiracy, the new religion of disbelief, the new heroism of evasion and blank rage. Between the quick cuts and the truncated guitar licks there was barely time to educate a viewer presumed to be too stoned to grasp much beyond a loosely structured paranoid lyricism. A diagrammatic cinema was required to spell out the hierarchies and chains of command of techno-industrial society. This is the way things really work: the police (*Serpico, Confessions of a Police Captain*), the Mafia (*The Godfather II, The Family*), the government (*All the President's Men, The Private Files of J. Edgar Hoover*). This is the way World War II really happened: *Patton, Tora! Tora! Tora!, Cross of Iron.* History could now be revealed not as a platform for solo heroics but as the implacable grinding of an infernal machine, from the slavery days of *Mandingo* to the unavoidable programmed future already on display in *A Clockwork Orange.* The real melodrama of politics made it to the screen for the first time: cool, analytical, and decentered, designy and hard-hearted like a spaghetti western. Everything you've ever been told was disinformation planted by the conspiratorial elite that controls absolutely everything except (through some thoroughly inexplicable oversight) the movie you are watching: *The Conversation, Three Days of the Condor, The Parallax View, The Domino Principle, Executive Action.*

At the theater down the street, porno. After Vietnam the wave of hard-core washed up on every drive-in screen in America. The old genres—the rusted cowboy pictures and spy thrillers and now-it-can-be-told war stories—could not be discarded fast enough to make way for the new show: Fellatio Comes to Elmtown. Splotched distended genitals beamed into the night of the middle country amid the fluttering of moths and the howling of a distant guard dog.

To go up against the novelties of porn—frontal nudity, penetration, the "money shot"—required a comparably fresh encounter with other aspects of the body's fate. It took creative forms of torture and dismemberment, flesh-eating zombies munching on actual intestines, a layer of skin being torn away on screen. Or black gangsters enacting Byzantine power struggles in the inner city, or kung fu avengers delivering the thunder kick to murderous capitalists, or Clint Eastwood letting loose an obliterating barrage with his Magnum .44. Anything to show that this was not the same old picture. No more Glenn Ford or Hope Lange, no more Henry Mancini music, no more happy ending. Rough and pitiless the way you secretly always wanted them to be: Saturday-night entertainment for mercenaries and pirates.

No major adjustments had to be made in deep plot structure. The grammar worked the way it always had. Merely rearrange a few markers, switch the goal posts. This time the good guys lose. The thieves get away with the money. The girl is not rescued but murdered. The cop didn't save anybody, he set them up in the first place. The babysitter wants to destroy the family. The government investigator was assassinated because he found out that the government did it. The monsters have taken over the world, they changed their faces so nobody would know. THE END is not a resolution but a trigger for future disorder. The charred corpse winks. The killer will come back. The virus has not really been eradicated.

IT IS ALWAYS the present. It is always dissolving. The water writing splits apart. "Now" is an unstable element in which the brand-new is prerecorded and yet will not be broadcast until a tomorrow that by the time the next issue of *Entertainment Weekly* comes out will already be ancient. *Big Bad Mama II* (once again the early-bird special on cable this morning) is both forever young and forever out of date. Every spectator becomes a floating free-lance media analyst, rehashing career moves of forgotten careers, taking inventory of outmoded hats and hemlines, registering the belated offensiveness of twenty-year-old one-liners. The cinematic graph of decay asserts itself as the most precise and merciless measurement of the passage of time.

Even when the new is newest you are already too aware by long experience of how rapidly it will become the past. They are born old: the computerized ballistics tests and android pectorals, the approximations of payload and nuclear devastation, the comedies about toxic waste and sexually predatory mutants, the laser-generated remakes of *Gunga Din* and *The Adventures of Captain Marvel* as stridently optimistic as promotional shorts at an auto retailers' sales convention, the feature-length commercials for soda and airplanes punctuated by spasms of sleekly crafted flaying and disembowelment. An exploding head, a can of Pepsi, and you. Design a more realistic simulation of bursting entrails and the world will beat a path to your door, but by the time it gets there it will have forgotten why it came and what it's doing standing around trying to buy some popcorn in time for the feature presentation.

The decades slid by so quickly in the dark. What year was it, anyway, and in which of the worlds you'd lived in simultaneously? A life spent watching movies could best be described by certain movie titles: *A Double Life, I Died a Thousand Times,*

I've Lived Before. Caught up in the shifting celluloid waters, living in reverse and playback, you ended up craving an anchor, something that had definitely happened at a definite time, a Great Real Thing providing ballast for the phantoms. Could anything real be inscribed on those liquid surfaces, anything harsh and durable? If you could find your way back to it you could trace another route, a road on which the world could be seen truly as it was.

orpheus and his brothers

There had been a war, the source of what was real, as real as a bullet preserved in a drawer or a photograph of an open grave. It provided a basis for comparison. Taking that as point of origin you could sort out fact from dream, truthful movies (those that remembered the war) from false movies (those that denied it had happened).

In the world the war had made, reality was in black-and-white. Color was suitable for candy wrappers, comic books, and Maria Montez vehicles. Within their secret economy where reds and golds were bartered, the children lusted after color: the satiny purples and gleaming golds of *Samson and Delilah*, the suffused green draperies and opalescent gems of *Cobra Woman*, the palpable slate-blue skies and desert lightning of *She Wore a Yellow Ribbon*. Color was sex. Color was money. Color was God.

The grown-ups meanwhile were abandoned to the black-and-white domain of bombarded cities and politicians under investigation for bribe-taking and atomic espionage, to a tonality that guaranteed the absence of miracles. No soft soap or happy endings, no chance to give it the Hollywood treatment. Here married couples quarreled out of habit, men in undershirts on hot summer nights drank beer and lashed out under the influence of murderous boredom, women lost their ability to make breakfast or stop sobbing and were taken away somewhere, soldiers failed even in the last reel to return from the rehab center.

Was it in that same grainy place that the photographs in *The Family of Man* had been taken, each picture a certificate of realness? Or the haunting picture in *Life* magazine that might have been either a snapshot of a ruined city or a still from one of the postwar Italian movies, *Open City, Paisan, The Bicycle Thief, Shoeshine*? Something harsh had managed to break through the protective barrier of advertisements for refrigerators and station wagons. Ragged children sat on a curb. A passionate woman screamed at a policeman. Drunkards declared that the war was over before being killed by a leftover land mine. Survivors sold bread and radio parts among gutted train stations and torn wall posters.

An American child might look at such pictures as if to be instructed in the meaning of "hunger" and "pain." The effect was beautiful, not horrifying. The pictures were peculiarly reassuring, as if the fact that someone could cry out made the world a nobler place. You felt better, as if you had become part of a larger humanity by responding to the plight of foreign beggars and orphans.

There was life in the ruins, a rusted rotting life, menacing and erotic. Hard-faced young thugs in tight jackets, the war children, lay in ambush for off-duty GIs and dreamed of owning motorcycles. At least half the planet appeared to be under an American occupation that promoted jazz, cowboy movies, and prostitution. Whatever sense of public space existed was linked to the pageantry of cut-rate floor shows, primitive replicas of El Morocco or the Copacabana. Emaciated glue-sniffers hung around the kitchen door hoping for scraps. There was plenty of money to be made off black-market tires or contraband penicillin. Along the margins, for the benefit of the children and the old people, a makeshift culture of street entertainers sprang up: clowns, storytellers, weight lifters, string bands. They painted posters by hand in what were still homemade neighborhoods.

As for the officials—the cops, the bureaucrats—they were cautiously regrouping, arranging to have their files purged or their names changed. A few social workers ventured into the shanty towns to reclaim delinquent war orphans. Homes for victims occasionally featured benevolent nurses and vases of flowers. In the name of reconstruction, whores were taken off the street and permitted to remember their childhood. They were going to build a playground on the site of the devastated interrogation center. A chorus of locals—variously maimed, bereft, tipsy, or conniving—chimed in with salty commentary, rich dialect humor at the expense of all people in uniforms. The young would have none of it. They were too busy combing their hair and listening to mambo music on a stolen radio.

It all had to do with a world that was trying to stitch itself back together, a world that wanted demonstrations of concern. Children were taken on tours of the United Nations and were told how famous musicians, sculptors, and movie actors had contributed to the cause of global peace. Out of the ashes, out of the rubble, something new was being born. It was art. It healed. At the Venice Film Festival it spoke a language of universally shared gestures and textures, a dialect of mud puddles and thatch and tears equally understandable in Italy and Sweden and California, India and Brazil and Japan.

Torrents, for instance. The grain of the film registered the weight and soddenness of the rain as it poured down on the deserted temple in *Rashomon* and again on the hapless father and son adrift in the slums of *The Bicycle Thief* and again on the Indian villagers of *Pather Panchali,* the Sicilian fishermen of *La Terra Trema,* the wandering mountebanks of *La Strada,* the Mexican street urchins hardened beyond caring in *Los Olvidados.* The film festival provided a vehicle for differences which seemed increasingly like similarities, as if Sicily and Mexico and Bengal were located in the same neighborhood, an exotic place where things were authentic. A context was created in which the spectacle of poverty could function as an aesthetic object. It was all so beautifully photographed.

Peasants, urban slum dwellers, displaced persons. They suffered, they rebelled—there was a period of exaltation and wild gaiety, lending itself to exuberant displays of camera technique and festive music on the soundtrack—and then by an inexorable mechanism their rebellion was suppressed. They inherited tragedy, and it was tragedy that made possible the great cinematic moments when the camera offered up their pain as the medium for a curiously liberating experience. The child died, the strikers were shot down, the innocent were abandoned to the noisy indifference of the big city. You had been waiting all through the movie to experience that moment of genuine feeling.

You became a vicarious inhabitant of those streets out there, an urban fugitive like Richard Widmark in *Night and the City* or James Mason in *Odd Man Out,* dying finally like a dog just as morning light filled the shattered street. Only a mute and apparently disinterested child was at hand to witness it: a harshly ironic contrast, beautifully photographed. It certainly wasn't *Seven Brides for Seven Brothers,* this range of ten thousand distinguishable monochrome textures, stippled and variegated like rare fabrics or ancient mosaics: wounds and rags, the faces of the sick and the tortured.

When people died here they stayed impressively dead: unless it was *Ugetsu* and the dead woman reappeared to welcome her husband back from his tortuous journey, or *The Seventh Seal* and all the plague victims joined hands in silhouette to do the Dance of Death, or *Orpheus* and the dead walked in and out of mirrors when they weren't communicating over car radios. For there was a reverse side to Film Art: if one face was uncompromisingly real, without cosmetics or studio orchestras, the other opened on the dreamlike and fantastic, like that succession of medieval microcosms (*Beauty and the Beast, Ivan the Terrible, The Seventh Seal*) sculpted out of light and cloth.

CIVILIZATION COULD BE defined as the areas within which there were theaters devoted exclusively to these movies. In New York City, for example, the Thalia, the 57th Street Playhouse, the Bleecker Street Cinema: temples whose enshrined saints were Eisenstein, Pabst, Welles, von Sternberg, Cocteau, Rossellini, Kurosawa, Bergman. That it was a religion was clear from the quiet intensity of the old men who came night after night, who had decades ago actually conversed with Dietrich or von Stroheim, who knew which shots were missing in the available prints of *Intolerance* or *The Battleship Potemkin*.

The dialogue emerged fitfully out of lobby smoke: "For Dietrich the essential one was the train . . ." "*Shanghai Express.*" "Exactly. Colin Clive . . ." "No, Clive Brook, my friend." "Clive Brook. Warner Oland. 'It took more than one man to change my name to Shanghai Lily.' " "But wait a minute, my friend, you're forgetting the ape suit . . ." "*Blonde Venus.*" " 'Hot Voodoo.' " " 'Hot Voodoo.' Ah . . ." The speaker relapses into a sigh encompassing all earthly joys and sorrows. But only for an instant before it resumes again, the dialogue that can end only with death.

Beyond those restricted precincts, the films were known only insofar as periodically some were given wider distribution bearing new titles like *The Young and the Passionate, The Young and the Damned, The Proud and the Beautiful, This Strange Passion, The Strange Ones,* announced by newspaper ads and posters featuring beautiful women in black negligees or standing knee-deep in rice paddies. The wider impact of Italian Neorealism could be summed up in a single proposition: "That Silvana Mangano is some broad."

Which was another way of saying that she or any of the other newly revealed foreigners represented the promise of a different life, the timeless village, the hotel room in the exotic city. Or rather, she simply lived that alternative life and you were privileged to see it happen. To call Anna Magnani an icon was insufficient. Icons do not laugh or commandeer a side street with a tilt of the shoulder. You watched her living some of the most important moments of her life. You had to believe that: it wasn't acting. It was a gift she bestowed. Feeling was set adrift on an electric current. It reached you in the form of trapped particles of light.

The seriousness of the rite was clear from the outset. No wonder the Catholic Church tried to ban Magnani's performance as the possessed peasant woman in *The Miracle,* raped by a stranger on the mountain and making her way through the wilderness to give birth to God. It was a primitive enactment of sacred madness actually being filmed. The camera of Rossellini became ancient and numinous by virtue of what it focused on. It wasn't something that happened *then*—it was happening right now, in the screening room, an inner surrender to this particular incarnation of the divine. The God-force was not precisely in front of the camera, nor in it, nor on the other side of it. It lay somehow in the relation among all those elements. Rossellini succeeded in making even the uncomfortable folding seats into pews for the reception of spirit.

There was a band of them, men now old or dead who had made the camera an instrument for photographing the invisible. The Frenchman Bresson, who framed the almost empty faces of nonprofessional actors as if they were bait for trapping a state of grace. The Dane Dreyer, who stared so relentlessly at his people that it seemed he could follow them into death and then bring them back, like the young woman lying dead at the end of *Ordet* who resurrected on camera, as if to say it was just that simple: you watched for it in stillness and it happened, without fanfare or gasps from a crowd of extras. The Japanese Mizoguchi, who moved his camera in beguiling and enveloping patterns that blocked out magical boundary lines, like the protective ideograms that the Buddhist monk painted all over the bewitched hero of *Ugetsu*. Mizoguchi's camera could move through space and time, insinuating a passageway between their seams and reversing them, like a pocket turned inside out. In a single 360-degree maneuver in *Ugetsu,* the camera swept past a cold empty corner of an abandoned house and circled back to find a dead woman tending a fire in the identical spot.

It was the simplest of magic, the trick being that there was no trick. Rossellini carried it as far as it could go. The lens simply allowed itself to be filled by a statement the world made. This is a tree. This is an elephant. This is a hill. This is Saint Francis in ecstasy. This is barbed wire. This is a woman stepping out of a car. This is a woman stepping out of her life. This is congealed lava. This is random light.

It had taken a long time for it to emerge into open air, like a splinter working its way back to the surface of the skin, this final cultural by-product of the murderous process that had been modern Europe. You witnessed that history by steeping yourself in the films. *A Nous la Liberté, The Blue Angel, M, La Grande Illusion, Alexander Nevsky, Day of Wrath:* they were wall paintings that flickered and spoke, on whose cracked and dingy surfaces a series of already ancient massacres could be traced. In a luminous handwriting that could never be duplicated, the Berlin of 1931 or the Paris of 1937 or the occupied Denmark of 1942 spelled itself out.

Possibilities remained open. The plump and nervous burgh-
ers of *M,* with their newspapers and meerschaum pipes, had
not yet voted for Hitler. There was still an open road where
the merry vagabonds of *A Nous la Liberté* could escape from
industrialists and policemen and rich men's daughters. The
policemen and professors and whores and pickpockets inhabited a society preparing to erase itself. In battered 16-millime-
ter prints they paced the limits of their tinny, splotched eternity, oblivious to the end of the reel. It was like watching, in
slow motion, the prelude to a car crash.

The men behind the camera must have known they were
caught in a trap. Why else would Fritz Lang have divided his
universe into cubbyholes, why else would he frame his child-
murderer—the one who would cry out, "I want to escape
from myself but I can't!"—against a circular maze spinning
ceaselessly in the window of a toy shop? The Europeans made a
graph of the city where the doors were rat holes and where
convoys of police cars formed interesting geometric configurations as they sped from headquarters. Desire retreated into
smoky confined culs-de-sac and cluttered, glittering music-hall
dressing rooms: the female underworld governed by Louise
Brooks. The rooms were too small, the movements too precisely calibrated. Nobody could move across the screen without making a pattern.

While they were waiting they listened to music, they
danced, they sang. The records spinning on the gramophones
symbolized love's recurrences, the seasons of life, the endless
repetition of the same set of powerless feelings. Accordions,
mandolins, gypsy violins, out-of-tune pianos, sour trumpets
blaring imitation Dixieland: these held open the last exit. The
camera was never more at home with itself than when it fas-

tened on Isa Miranda or Lili Damita or Zarah Leander in the heart of her song. It had found something that everyone could live with, for as long as closing time could be kept at bay.

This was the Europe in which it would remain 1929 forever. The recurrence of a tango melody—by accident, from a radio or the window of a phonograph shop—delivered lovers from suicide and unemployment. Each ran as if by instinct toward the train station, the junction where destinies would be sorted out. In the harbor the fog cleared just long enough to permit the departure of a steamer bound for Caracas.

And outside the film studios, in the wideness and bareness of nature, what pictures of happiness they had made—Jean Renoir, René Clair, Jean Vigo, Max Ophuls—as they mapped out places of refuge in the meadows and canals of the early sound period. They were teaching the camera how to breathe, how to take its time and linger over changes of mood, changes of light, changes in the weather. They were beginning to uncover the stretches of beach and marshland where lovers and artists and proletarians could be safe even from narrative. They only needed a few more years, a few more minutes.

ALONG THE PERIMETERS of the fully electric world of gramophones and luxury cinemas, other men were rehearsing another more traditional kind of knowledge, of precisely how men were to be trussed up before being burned, of how their faces would look when pleading or at the exact moment when they abandoned all attempt at pleading. Sergei Eisenstein, in *Alexander Nevsky,* could convincingly film German atrocities on Russian soil before they were even committed. For a Hollywood-educated American viewer, the movie was at once initiation and replay, a born-again Errol Flynn movie with the debonair Flynn replaced by the autocratic Nikolai Cherkassov. Cherkassov was a *serious* hero with no time or inclination for swashbuckling antics, not even a girl to kiss. He was lord of a land without mercy, with the streak of unforgiving cruelty necessary for confronting Germans in horned helmets who were scary in a way that Basil Rathbone or Claude Rains never could be. Sardonic witticisms were alien to these Teutonic invaders. They were simply the presence of death.

Alien and utterly familiar, *Alexander Nevsky* somehow consecrated the stock routines and props of the adventure movie. For once they assumed their innate significance and importance: the armor, the lances, the hooves pounding across the ice as the music thumped energetically in cadence, the clashes and lunges and heroic wounds. To share the exhilaration of the whole Russian people climbing out of their hovels or homesteads, trudging across sands and over hills in ever larger bands as the music grew correspondingly louder and fuller and more heart-stirring . . . to identify with the quiet but absolutely unbendable strength of Nevsky, dressed in down-to-earth fisherman's clothes on his first appearance . . . to surrender entirely to sadness and awe as during the night after the battle the Russian women walked across the ice with torches, searching among the dead and dying for their fallen: here was an incomparable education in patriotic joys and sorrows, a rehearsal for the business of war.

Then it all had to move indoors, underground, hide out on painted sets, in masks and costumes: production during wartime, when what was not shown weighed on the visible. German martial law encompassed the Danish soundstage where in 1943, in Carl Dreyer's *Day of Wrath,* actors dressed up as black-robed church elders probed the back of an old woman with pins looking for the devil's mark so they could consign her to the flames. Within Stalin's closed world Sergei Eisenstein created another closed world as he choreographed the torch flares, processions, and slow-motion assassinations of *Ivan the Terrible.* (The actor enthroned amid *Ivan's* baroque catacombs, Nikolai Cherkassov again, was a spy for Stalin, managing to keep an eye on the director even as he was momentarily pinioned by Eisenstein's geometrics.)

THE WAR WAS fought so that Europeans could become human again, so they could break out of a world defined by overdecorated sets and camera setups as rigidly formalized as wedding cakes. The British were halfway there, in the war but not conquered, and even years after the war was over it was possible to feel it was still being fought in the perfectly preserved frames of *The Way Ahead* and *We Dive at Dawn* and *In Which We Serve.* The hieratic structure of a fighting unit was modified to incorporate an undercurrent of tender comradeship and sober mutual respect.

What was reassuring about the English movies was the matter-of-fact way they diagrammed how organizations worked. After the war that aesthetic of the training film would expand into a vision of bureaucratic benevolence coping with the problems of economic hardship and petty crime. The policemen of *The Blue Lamp* and the policewomen of *Both Sides of the Law* labored with anonymous heroism in a system where every copper and clerk and ordinary eyewitness played a part in keeping the whole machine functioning. Here was a society where lost bicycles were not stolen as in Neorealist Italy, but returned, mended almost like new. (By extension, America was a society where lost bicycles were instantly replaced by new ones, and Russia was a society where bicycles did not exist.)

Whatever residue lay outside that very British grid was Poetry, a zone of bonus pleasures: the childish and fantastic undertones that so lovingly informed *The Fallen Idol* and *Dead of Night* and *Stairway to Heaven,* or the glistening and mildly erotic historical surfaces of *Saraband for Dead Lovers* and *Fanny by Gaslight.* The English movies conveyed a sense of precision and control. You would be shown exactly what you needed to see to make sense of what was going on, with no loose ends. This was an approach peculiarly apt for giving credence to uncanny premonitions (*Interrupted Journey*), richly ironic twists of fate (*Train of Events*), and surprise visitations from otherworldly Scotland Yard investigators (*An Inspector Calls*).

THE HARDER YOU looked for truth in those images the more they transformed themselves into dreams. Not just the movies that acknowledged their illusoriness, like *The Red Shoes* and *An American in Paris:* all movies behaved like that, most especially the ones that pretended not to know that anybody was watching them. You were drawn ever deeper into a hermetic hall of mirrors, getting in so deep it seemed that only movies could get you out.

Around 1960 something shifted; the glassy surface began to

crack. That year three movies announced, as if it had been a concerted effort, the approaching breakdown of the screen as barrier: the Voyeur Trilogy, consisting of Alfred Hitchcock's *Psycho,* Michael Powell's *Peeping Tom,* and Fritz Lang's *The Thousand Eyes of Dr. Mabuse.* It was as if someone behind the screen were cutting a hole in it, like the hole in the wall through which Anthony Perkins spied on Janet Leigh in her motel room. (Hitchcock's production note for the shower scene read: "An impression of a knife slashing, as if tearing at the very screen, ripping the film.") *Peeping Tom,* which was about a movie camera that killed as it filmed, hooked itself into the spectator's world in rigorous fashion: the first shot was an enormous close-up of an open eye, the last consisted of an empty screen with the projector's noise on the soundtrack.

In the Lang movie—his last—all the characters lived inside a house of eyes, the Hotel Luxor, whose secret was revealed when the camera tracked back from a couple conversing at a table in the dining room—moved back as if passing into a different medium, to reveal the same image appearing on a television screen. "Up there! Television cameras! They're all over the hotel! Everywhere, in every room! In the bar, in the restaurant, in the nightclub! They see everything!" Dawn Addams pointed and the camera obliged by showing close-ups of little holes staring blankly back at the lens.

It was just another episode in Fritz Lang's forty-year serial, now nearly ended—or more precisely suspended. He could have stopped right there, left the camera running for twelve hours or twelve years on the little camera eye staring from its hiding place in the wall, a means of communication communicating nothing whatsoever. It might have been a last warning smuggled from Dr. Mabuse's headquarters: *The wall is watching you. You are being filmed.*

Until there was nothing to do but infiltrate the reality factory and bring back a movie of how the movie was being made. Never mind technique: hand-held camera and natural light would do, and a shopping cart or a wheelchair for dolly shots. The new movies admitted that they were there and that you were watching them. The image *had* to wobble, to prove it was really shot in someone's backyard. The acorns were not props. The girl was a real girl and not Betty Grable. A passing truck drowned out the dialogue in order to provide further verification of authenticity.

The studio movies had emanated from an unapproachable hermetic zone. The new people (Jean-Luc Godard, François Truffaut, John Cassavetes, Shirley Clarke, Richard Leacock) smuggled equipment outside. Hitherto it had been forbidden to photograph the way things looked; people were not allowed to scratch themselves or go without makeup. And now here it all was—and that was enough. It didn't matter if, in *Breathless,* Jean Seberg and Jean-Paul Belmondo spent half an hour of screen time in a hotel room barely wide enough to give the camera space to turn around in. Everybody was in there with them, appreciating that the place was really there: and that was Paris out the window, not a movie of Paris. Why had people spent half a century photographing fake things?

THE LINK BETWEEN the old world and the new was a shot of Belmondo posing beside a poster of Humphrey Bogart in *The Harder They Fall.* How strange to see a movie poster in a movie, and to see the French actor imitating (with overemphatic deliberation) the American actor's effortless gesture, as if the goal were to make difficult what had hitherto been easy. The simplest actions—how to mount a horse, how to grab someone's lapels during an argument—would have to be rethought from scratch. Nothing could ever again be perfectly natural. So that Bogart (or Cooper, or Gable) became in the celluloid afterlife a disembodied tutelary spirit of unselfconscious behavior. What could still be seen of Bogart—the quantifiable rhythms and reflexes, the rictus of his grin, the business of tugging on his ear—was nonetheless as irretrievable as the despoiled innocence of the natives in a South Seas picture.

So—by this circuitous route—the more direct and honest it got, the more detached, ironic, and frankly fake it was forced to become. "We are so open we can show how closed we are." The primitive action picture evolved into a grainy, jittery documentary about European intellectuals pretending to be hit men or cowboys. Nature had been America, and America was dead. From its corpse the outlanders made a shrine in which the humblest fragments—a long shot of a cattle drive underscored by Hans Salter, a pan across neon bar fronts in an Allied Artists second feature—achieved a solemnity they had never possessed in life. In the new sect that was reaffirming the religion of cinema, the chief rite consisted of reenacting what had already been filmed, an Eternal Return of the beloved melodramas.

Because (and here lay its hidden joy) this modern Nature could be resurrected at will. It all still lived, the old films breathed anew at each projection. The young cinéastes could inhabit the inner respiration of *True Heart Susie* and *The Wedding March, The Passion of Joan of Arc* and *Steamboat Bill Junior, Gun Crazy* and *Stromboli* and *French Can Can* and *Mister Arkadin* and *Party Girl* and *Nosferatu,* over and over and over until their response went beyond visual memorization into a sort of Neoplatonic merging of the viewer and the viewed.

The life on the screen and the life in their bodies was one, after all. They confirmed that unity through an act of unqualified surrender, and like all mystics came back from the experience able to speak only in cryptic and paradoxical utterances, oblique allusions to what passes understanding. ''When I talk about ideas, I really mean ideas . . . of framing or the way shots are put together, which these days are the only ideas whose profundity I wish to recognize''—Jacques Rivette. ''One is no longer interested in objects, but in what lies between the objects and becomes an object in its turn''—Jean-Luc Godard. ''The true is as false as the false, and only the ultra-false becomes true''—Luc Moullet. ''There is alarm over the disappearance of sacred art: what does it matter, if the cinema is taking over from the cathedrals!''—Eric Rohmer.

Nowhere was this faith practiced more fervently than in the austere atmosphere of the Cinémathèque Française in Paris, where a band of spectators could sit silent and immobile for six hours as one of Louis Feuillade's crime serials, *Les Vampires* or *Judex* or *Tih Minh,* unreeled without musical accompaniment or spoken commentary, with only the occasional intertitle to establish the context: The Bleeding Wall. The Gem That Kills. The Mysterious Shadow. The Eyes That Fascinate. Among the Mad. The Mysteries of the Villa Circe. The shuttered roadster sped inexorably along the corniche. The conspiratorial anarchists danced in smoky taverns. Drugged nuns wandered through a landscaped garden. Men in black masks disappeared through trapdoors and alleyways.

And then, as if between the seams of the intrigue, the camera stumbled upon the street, the sky, the ocean. The air of 1915 leaked into the screening room. Not a whisper or a sigh betrayed any audience response: that would already have been excessive. The core of the experience, its sole reward, was an unvoiced inward sense of completion. "Whatever is, is": these were the only words that Jacques Rivette, in the pages of *Cahiers du Cinema,* could find for such an encounter.

What were you doing as you sat in the dark? You were seeing what had been put there—by the director or by God. In the crisscrossing patterns of Murnau and Hitchcock you discerned theorems of an occult mathematics, a Kabbalah of diagonals and encirclements. The movie was at all times saying more than it said it was. With its colors and geometries it invaded language. The takeover was silent and total. The actors, and the dialogue they spoke, could hardly grasp what they were enveloped in, or what that larger space was that deigned to let them exist inside it.

Yes, but what were you *doing*? Seeing. Feeling. Meditating. Thinking? Not quite as thinking had been understood in the past. You weren't so much enumerating things or breaking them down or solving the problems their interrelations provoked as you were appreciating, wordlessly, the way they fit together. Meaning could wait. For the moment, in the dark, you had no choice but to turn off the analysis machine and let things be. It was as close as you would ever come to the people who sat for centuries on church pews, for whom stained glass and organ loft had anticipated, however inadequately, the function of wide screen and studio orchestra.

They had sat there so patiently for so long, making do with faint prefigurations. For millennia the world had been waiting for the birth of the movies.

ghost opera

What did people do, anyway, before there were movies?

BY THE RAYS of the sun or by wavering firelight they traced inked shapes. They sounded them in the air with their voices. They pulled strings to move puppets or spin tops. They draped rags over their heads and assumed the voices of kings or ghosts or serving maids.

They carved faces in trees or pumpkins. They nicked, seared, gouged, sprinkled, wove, daubed, wrapped, folded, scratched. They sang. They hummed. They whistled. They plucked and pounded and blew. They whooped, they jumped. They banged on a cask to make an echo like thunder.

They peered at tiny moving things: rivers of drops, emergent larvae, molten wax. They made bets on how long it would take an object to melt or burn up. They smelled the bridge, the shells, the rope. The night made noises. Smoke was altered by rain. The weather made the world different every time it shifted. They studied the rate at which things changed.

The darkness was filled with names and rhymes, hoots and thumps, catechisms and soliloquies. By day due note was taken of scars and griefs and epitaphs. Somebody had once seen a play with a horse in it, or had been told of a battle. Extended reveries might be initiated by handling a remnant of someone else's life, a pipe, a candlestick, a bundle of letters. Dramas were buried in words ("liberty" or "revenge") and clothes (a cape, a pair of boots). There was endless play in sticks, buttons, cracked rocks, fallen trees. They hid. Shadows made rooms for them.

THEN THEY MADE rooms for shadows and for a hundred years everybody went to the movies.

IT TOOK A considerable while to build the shadow machines. Scientists and entrepreneurs and amateur visionaries experimented with wheels and gelatin and beams of light. They spent the better part of the nineteenth century getting the show ready. In the meantime people looked at pictures, enormous gilt-framed canvases that covered whole walls, big enough to put the Andes and the Alps and the Rocky Mountains in your lap.

They might wait in line for hours to catch a glimpse of a single such painting: a panorama of tropical swamps giving way to an endless succession of scooped-out glaciated rock forms, white crags extending all the way to heaven. The painter had spent a year preparing these caves and trails for them to voyage in. It was a major production, sketched on location and realized with the best material resources money could buy.

The rest of the time they looked at pictures of pictures: lithographs, cartoons, sketches, posters, broadsides, paintings on church walls or wagons or cracker boxes, pictures of clowns and notorious murderers and an actress strapped to the back of a wild horse in a dramatization of Byron's *Mazeppa*. Nuns cast their eyes downward in modest ecstasy. An Oriental tyrant prepared to massacre his own harem. A maiden gathered flowers. A mischievous urchin squirmed to evade a well-deserved spanking.

They had been taught to look into the eyes of the portrait to catch the depth of feeling the painter had put there. They grasped intuitively the weight of the instant when the brush tip made contact with the blank canvas. They had been primed by countless stories about painters, Florentine painters, Parisian painters, lovesick painters, roguish painters, blissful God-struck painters, vengeful painters—and stories about models, their lithe comeliness and easy morals and wasting illnesses, and stories about unfinished masterpieces and artists driven mad by the intensity of their inner visions, and stories about the hauntings and lingering curses that could attach themselves to pictures and wreak havoc on the unwary connoisseur.

Sooner or later they saw every scene they could ever have imagined. A Moorish executioner stood astride the steps at whose base a severed head rolled. Privileged voluptuous women inhabited spacious atria and seraglios. Victims of plague and shipwreck died in plain sight. A gypsy girl danced for pennies in a Neapolitan alley. Armies of conquering Turks seized control of harbors and temples. Lava overwhelmed the sybarites of Herculaneum. The earth opened, the typhoon smashed the fishing fleet. Terrified heretics were delivered into the hands of hooded inquisitors. Lions chewed over the entrails of martyrs. Tiny naked sinners cowered in the face of the deluge. In its last hour the universe exploded in whorls of judgment. Each isolated picture was so powerful that it was hard to imagine what might result from making it move, and then yoking together a succession of such moving pictures: more excitement, perhaps, than the human frame could long sustain.

THE NEW ERA might be said to have begun on May 9, 1893, when members of the Brooklyn Institute of Arts and Sciences lined up to peep into Thomas Edison's Kinetoscope and watch a twenty-second film of three men hammering on an anvil and sharing a bottle of beer. Or perhaps December 28, 1895, when at the Grand Café in Paris the Lumière brothers inaugurated a program featuring *The Arrival of a Train at the La Ciotat Station* and other movies made with a camera-projector-printer called a cinematograph. The spectators' eyes adjusted to what they didn't know was a new species of language. It had begun to alter them even before they had a name for it.

A toy, a peepshow, a scientific novelty: something small-scale and manageable. Neither Edison nor the Lumière brothers nor the other hardheaded capitalists and dogged tinkerers who got movies off the ground could have foreseen the depths of the fascination their machinery would provoke, or that a century later a whole planet would remain transfixed by its simulation of vital movement. The medium might evolve, becoming a multitude of different media in the process; but like one-celled organisms, *Blacksmith Scene* or *Workers Leaving the Lumière Factory* already contained the essential. What followed was just a matter of accretion and technological fine-tuning.

The story was never done being told because it wasn't finished yet. Every new plot development in the story of movies forced a revision of all earlier accounts of the beginning. If an earlier model of film history went from the twenty-second one-shot movie to *Intolerance,* the newest might go from *This Is Cinerama* to the music video and the twenty-second TV commercial. The story of movies had been, at various times and places, a story of technological progress; of a sensation in the vaudeville business; of society overrun by seductive images of vice; of art and science collaborating harmoniously to produce a universal medium; of solitary film geniuses purifying a language of gesture and visual rhythm; of radical visionaries seizing the means of production in order to deprogram the brainwashed masses; of multinational corporations conspiring to reassert control over all forms of electronic communication.

What was the current reading, the unfinished and indeterminate one? It began to look like a story of unforeseeable viruslike proliferation. A small gadget capable of showing a single flickering scene became the global environment. It exercised a strange attraction over all who came into its vicinity, until in the end they wanted to be not merely the spectators but the spectacle that was being watched. To that end they strove to turn their lives into moving pictures, their wars into moving pictures, their governments into moving pictures. (Power could be redefined as the force guaranteeing that the show would keep on going: "Vote for me or there won't be any more television.") Not an utterly paranoid interpretation, if information theorists were correct in finding close similarities between patterns of viral infection and the way information diffused and mutated.

In 1905 people stepped into nickelodeons to encounter the novel excitement of a disordered, constantly shifting world of pratfalls, state funerals, heroic firemen, and scenic tours. The world had not changed yet, there was simply a new way to get a glimpse of it. The "nickel madness"—an addiction to frittering away more and more time sitting in the dark watching *Hypnotist's Revenge* and *The Snapshot Fiend* and *The Female Spy,* losing track of the hours, remaining transfixed as the program came full circle and began again—signaled the first great wave of enthusiasm for the new medium.

Since then the captive audience (no one talked much about their enthusiasm any more) had moved ever closer toward perceiving the world as an immense nickelodeon, an enclosed area delimited by walls of screens—movie screens, television screens, computer screens—on which the action never stops. Everybody's home address was now a decentered hyperspace swarming with random and infinitely reproducible images. Indeed, with the promise (or threat) of untold interactive modes and virtual realities, the race of viewers might be on the verge of taking the next step beyond spectatorship by entering the screen itself, like Buster Keaton in *Sherlock Junior.*

———

PEOPLE KEPT MAKING up a fiction, a myth, about the history of movies for the simplest of reasons: it happened to them, it happened to their family and their friends, it really mattered. There was a personal compulsion to make some sense of it. Movies were not "out there." They had long since been internalized by most humans on the planet—had been internalized, in a sense, even before the medium was invented. The germ of the idea went back centuries: or millennia, if you cared to retrace it to archaic stories about living shadows and deceptive visions, to the reflexive trap of Narcissus or Orpheus's backward glance.

You might, like the most thorough historical investigators, begin in the seventeenth century, with the magic lantern and with the German Jesuit Athanasius Kircher's treatise *The Great Art of Lights and Shadows*. It was Kircher who demystifed those optical tricks of reflection and enlargement—the magician's repertoire of mirrors and silhouettes—that had long been used to simulate the supernatural. As to how long such practices had been going on, Kircher ventured a reference to the time of King Solomon.

But how much farther back might you not trace that prehistory of projection, could you but find a surviving practitioner to initiate you? Was there a subculture of projectionists carefully guarding its technical secrets? Where were the lost slide shows of the Tibetans and the Olmecs? What had become of the medieval movies, the Graeco-Roman movies, the ancient Egyptian movies, or of the mystifying play of flame and shadow cast against cave walls to induce Cro-Magnon wonderment? Was that the sin for which Atlantis had been destroyed, not nuclear weapons after all, but the premature invention of

Technicolor and CinemaScope? Film would then only be a way of preserving on celluloid an art of optical deception that had existed for millennia, an art of blinks and smoke screens and sleight of hand: a hypnotic folk craft, preserved along with other such crafts only insofar as it could be translated into the impersonal grammar of industrial technology.

In any event the secret got out, and magic-lantern techniques passed from the realm of superstition to that of science; but the aura of the fantastic could not be shaken. In the late eighteenth and early nineteenth centuries, showmen staged elaborate lantern shows which offered to immerse the spectator in supernatural visions which were at the same time debunked. "This is a spectacle," declared one impresario, "which man can use to instruct himself in the bizarre effects of the imagination, when it combines vigor and derangement: I speak of the terror inspired by the shadows, spirits, spells, and occult work of the magician."

New York saw its first phantasmagoria exhibition in 1803, a "wonderful display of Optical Illusions" which paraded "the Phantoms, or Apparitions of the Dead and Absent," supposedly in order "to expose the practices of artful impostors and exorcists, and to open the eyes of those who still foster an absurd belief in *Ghosts or Disembodied Spirits.*" There was already a duality of intent: to create illusions and at the same time to lay bare the real. The audience was first of all to be terrified by apparitions, and afterward given a demonstration of the mobile glass slides and variable lanterns by which the illusion was produced.

The succeeding two centuries witnessed the gradual erosion of the supernatural through the combined effects of electric lights, photography, movies, and modern transportation. There were to be no more unlighted corners or inaccessible wilderness areas where ghosts and demons could congregate. An absolutely limited, purely material world registered on the lens of the camera. Before the emergence of the story film, actualities—street scenes, views from railroad carriages, parades, coronations, lifelike reenactments of crimes and battles—seemed to represent the medium's future.

Such a prognosis reckoned without an appetite for the fantastic that would persistently divert movies from the straightforward task of recording what was there. Upon the motion picture—the most alluring mechanism of the age of mechanical reproduction—would devolve the task of reconstructing the imaginary worlds it had helped to dismantle.

A FILM SCHOLAR—rational as such scholars must be, to keep from being driven mad by the materials they handle—divided the world of cinema into three domains, the technological, the socioeconomic, and the aesthetic. He could well have added a fourth: the religious. No previous medium having so vividly intimated the disappearance of God—there are sacred books but no sacred movies—it stood to reason that film would overcompensate by the systematic cultivation of visions, icons, exorcisms, martyrdoms, paradisiacal landscapes, and sacred rituals.

Sacred, or magical. Was this last inheritance of the nineteenth century one of those dangerous legacies that are regularly passed on in tales of the supernatural: keys to rooms never before opened, sealed vials of mysteriously potent liquids, ancient books containing necromantic inscriptions? For all the stolid workmanlike attitude of its inventors, movie technology fulfilled the most Faustian of ambitions.

At least two fin-de-siècle novels, *The Future Eve* (1880) by Villiers de l'Isle Adam and Jules Verne's *The Castle in the Carpathians* (1893), had anticipated a technology capable of generating simulacra indistinguishable from living humans. Villiers's Thomas Edison found it more convenient to substitute, for the real woman who had betrayed his best friend, an automaton indistinguishable from her and superior in every way. In Verne's more melancholy and unresolved book, a reclusive inventor coped with the death of his beloved by endlessly contemplating a hologram-like duplication of her, captured while she still lived. Such machines clearly had an infernal aspect. If man could no longer tell the difference between real and mechanical beings, then he fell prey to every kind of puppetry and deception. Lacking a clear definition of the word "human" meant losing the basis for moral judgments. The notion of "action" became equally problematic, since cinematic reproduction—an animate death—entailed a blurring of just what constituted the present moment.

"When these cameras are made available to the public," wrote a journalist in 1895, "when everyone can photograph their dear ones, no longer in a motionless form but in their movements . . . death will have ceased to be absolute." Or, in the words of the nineteenth-century scientist Georges Demeny: "The future will see the replacement of motionless photographs, frozen in their frames, with animated portraits that can be brought to life at the turn of a handle. . . . We will do more than analyze, we will *bring back to life.*" Hard not to think of the frenzied painter in Poe's *The Oval Portrait,* raving as he completed his uncannily lifelike picture of the wife who had died while sitting for him: "This is indeed *Life* itself!"

There was in fact a peculiar awe attendant upon watching the earliest movies. You looked not only at people who were dead but at a world that had disappeared: the world in which movies were unknown. You might be an extraterrestrial surveying the delayed signals from an already vanished planet. Yet the people moved about casually and did not know they were being transformed into a picture for the eyes of spectators yet unborn. They were being filmed but had not yet grasped what that implied. To intrude on that innocence could seem as much a violation as prying open a mummy case.

In the carnival tents, fairgrounds, music halls, and shopfronts where films were first exhibited, such metaphysical perplexities are unlikely to have been uppermost in viewers' minds. For those who peered at *Annabelle Serpentine Dance* or *The Boxing Cats* or *Chinese Laundry Scene,* through hand-cranked peepshows, or at the first flickering screen projections, the novelty of movement was enough. Clearly the first movies had nothing like the sustained hypnotic power of the narrative films that became dominant within ten years. What held the audience was not emotional involvement but amazement and curiosity. Fascination was learned behavior.

The spectator was still consciously comparing the images on the screen to what they were supposed to represent, so that filmed waves were described by a journalist as behaving "in the most natural manner." Such astonishment—at the simple fact of something, anything, being filmed—could not last very long. Once the initial shock was past, the movement of a wave

no longer sufficed. Entrancement by mere optical illusion became the subject of joke films, as in the 1902 *Uncle Josh at the
Moving Picture Show,* where a yokel tried to communicate with
the woman on the screen. (Godard would reinvent the joke
decades later in *Les Carabiniers,* as a lout from some unimaginable country without movies tried to clamber up on screen to
join a woman in her bathtub and succeeded only in ripping the
screen apart.)

A variety show of disconnected views with the exhibitor in
creative control, ''editing'' in deejay fashion through his mix
of one-shot subjects: that was the cinema supplanted by story
films like Griffith's, only to reemerge in the fragmented for-
mats of television and video. (There was even a promise of
wider and more inescapable diffusion in department stores and
bank lobbies and dentists' waiting rooms: open-ended twenty-
four-hour moving wallpaper without beginning or end.) Such
programs—interspersed with live entertainment—went after
contrast and diversity rather than coherent themes or moods.
It must have been something like a visual party.

And what did the spectators see? They saw bricks and
crockery, babies and dogs, chattering women and destructive
children, windows, sausages, a robber on stilts, a wife with a
rolling pin, banks, horse-drawn carriages, tramps, policemen,
wharves, ladders, grief-stricken widows and stolen children,
taverns, bottles of poison, telephones, railroad tunnels, escaped lunatics, armed anarchists, collapsing walls, acrobats,
flimflam artists, washerwomen, incomprehensible foreigners,
nursemaids with criminal tendencies, lecherous young men in
straw hats, modern girls smiling at the camera as their skirts
were blown up by the wind, comical bumpkins making a spec-

tacle of themselves on their visit to the big city.

And mixed indiscriminately with all that they saw pieces of real life. A fire breaking out in a warehouse; a cavalry troop charging; a battleship being launched; President McKinley speaking (without intertitles, a sublimely empty sight); the coffin of President McKinley lifted from a train; the assassin of President McKinley led from his cell, strapped into the electric chair, and executed.

This last was a reenactment, whether or not the audience knew it, any more than they knew that many of the "wargraphs" of the Spanish-American War were in varying degrees misrepresentations. The battleship shown was not really the *Maine;* the battleship shown was not really a battleship at all but a miniature; the battle shown "through the dense smoke" was a fake, with the smoke there to hide the traces of deception. Such frauds may well have advanced the range of techniques and textures, as filmmakers learned to imitate the look of documentary footage by making mistakes on purpose.

THE FILM BUSINESS was chaos, a battleground over kinds of property and kinds of freedom that hadn't yet been defined. Secret agents warred over cameras and projectors as over new types of weaponry, and the police kept a close eye on them when they weren't being paid off. As filmmakers poked around for subjects to point their cameras at—cooch dancers, boxing matches, cockfights, passion plays, representations of police brutality—they triggered unforeseen skirmishes.

The censorship fights raised curious philosophical problems. It was argued, for instance, that while boxing itself was illegal, a film of a boxing match, as a representation rather than the thing itself, was exempt from the law. Similarly, for an actor to play Jesus onstage was viewed as sacrilege. To make a film of an actor playing Jesus, however—and there was a wave of such films from 1897 on—could be construed as not only acceptable but inspirational.

The sacrilege of the stage Jesus lay in the fact that he was of flesh and blood; you might reach out and touch him; you might smell him. The figure on the screen belonged to a different order, odorless, and beyond touch: he was a phantasm, a trick of light. "There will be no 'real' actors," wrote the *Boston Herald* in 1898, "no living personages in the presentation of this most sacred and sublime of the world's tragedies." A clergyman testified that while "the performance of this play . . . by living actors and actresses was prohibited . . . to the rendition of it by these pictures there can be no objection."

So much for one theological take on film ontology. On the other hand, Pope Leo XIII consented to be filmed in Rome in 1898, and in the process bestowed a blessing directly on the camera filming him, as if the spiritual energy thus set loose could be canned in the apparatus, projected on the screen, and thereby transmitted to an audience on the other side of the Atlantic. The gesture implied a sort of cinematic transubstantiation.

Before Hollywood got a stranglehold on distribution, before the Hays Code cut back on controversy, people would and did try out anything. Ibsen, Schiller, companionate marriage, the Yellow Peril, capital punishment, female detectives: they all tumbled out so fast that there was no time or concern to sort them. Independents, even downright amateurs, still had a shot at getting in the game. The resulting cacophony—a traffic jam of moral uplift, unhinged propaganda, and enthusiastic exploitation—would be edited out in subsequent decades, largely through the mechanisms of self-censorship that took hold between the Fatty Arbuckle scandal of 1921 and the final imposition of the Production Code in 1934. In mainstream movies there would be no more revelations of drug addiction (*Human Wreckage*), birth control (*Where Are My Children?*), venereal disease (*Damaged Goods*), or prostitution (*Traffic in Souls, The House of Bondage,* and other instances of what *Variety* called "patchouli and kimono pictures").

IT WASN'T ONLY subject matter that changed. Someone who fell asleep in 1907, when D. W. Griffith was beginning his career at Biograph, and woke up in the 1920s would encounter a drastically streamlined world of complex feature-length stories, seamless editing, carefully crafted close-ups, fluid compositions and camera movements, subtly modulated lighting, and (sometimes) carefully synchronized live music, all framed by the glittering decor and precision-drill ushers of the dream palaces. As the opening title of von Sternberg's *The Last Command* declared: "Hollywood—1928! The Magic Empire of the Twentieth Century! The Mecca of the World!"

Above all the emotional relationship of the spectator to the screen had changed. There were movie stars, for one thing, a phenomenon driven not by producers but by audiences, who (as soon as close-ups showed the actors' faces clearly enough) recognized their favorites and made stars of them before they even knew their names: "The Biograph girl," "the Indian."

But people cared about the stars in large part because of the complex things that happened to them. Early story films—*The Great Train Robbery* (1903), *The Escaped Lunatic* (1903), *Rescued by Rover* (1905), *Automobile Thieves* (1906)—evolved out of physical actions that were easy to track: chases, abductions and recoveries, criminal attacks and police counterattacks. It took a decade of formal experiment to come up with ways of handling more complicated or more subtle plots.

The bumps that reminded you it was a movie had been smoothed. Nothing disturbed the reverie. In the 1920s, the director of a training school for movie-theater managers spelled it out in caressing prose: "People come to the motion picture theater to live an hour or two in the land of romance. . . . For a small charge they can be picked up on a magic carpet and set down in a dream city amidst palatial surroundings where worry and care can never enter, where pleasure hides in every colored shadow and music scents the air." Paramount touted its motion pictures in similar terms: "A magician somewhere waves his wand, and we're off on our travels into the realms of laughter and tears. . . . We are youthful romancers living in another world."

The pleasure of that escape became the most commonly shared pleasure of the century. Everybody could go into the same dark room—no matter where it happened to be located—and zero in on precisely the same dream. None of the noises and smells of circus or live theater; it was a more futuristic experience, the vision of the lone space traveler strapped down and watching the universe roll by outside his porthole. Narrative only offered a way in, a means of remaining in that intimate and trancelike space as long as possible.

That achieved dream voyage—the film art that triumphed in the 1920s—owed most to the audiences who, as children or adolescents, had watched the movies of the nickelodeon era and wondered. Some of those spectators were named Charlie Chaplin, F. W. Murnau, Fritz Lang, Ernst Lubitsch, Raoul Walsh, Josef von Sternberg, King Vidor, John Ford, Buster Keaton. The movies they made were a response to other movies: a dream replying to a dream.

Decades later it took only a small adjustment to reenter their world and allow the effect to take hold. With no dialogue to listen for, the eyes assumed complete control, learning to navigate the depths and rhythms of a universe of illuminated gestures. It was all utterly concrete. Only the visible existed, whether you were watching (in *Intolerance*) Constance Talmadge playfully biting a goat's ear or a series of razors poised to cut the rope that would hang a man.

But no matter how tightly the images were linked to a story line, the silence allowed leeway for each spectator's fantasy. The movie had to be met halfway, the viewer's imagination filling in the huge areas left unexpressed. The movie became an active dream, a waking trance cunningly orchestrated by visual musicians: a ghost opera, perfected just at the moment when synchronized sound was about to change everything yet again.

the author of the visible

For the first twenty years it was almost enough to show things. Robbers. Stenographers. Naughty children. Fires. Coronations. Battleships. More fires. People talking into telephones. Cars moving at high speed through narrow streets. The spectator wallowed in the visible like a neighbor perched on a stoop watching the world go by. There was a picnic of images. He picked one picture or another—a horse, an acrobatic maneuver, a winking eye—out of the unregulated current. "Look, the dog stole the man's sausages—the police are chasing him—the police fell on top of each other—and the dog ate up all the sausages—did you see that?" There was a satisfaction in being able to identify the elements of the story.

It was almost but not quite a sufficient thrill, that labor of recognizing who and what were being photographed and what they were up to. "Let's see, what's she going to do now? Something's up, that's clear. Looks like a suspicious type. Rob the till, is that the game?" Ultimately you needed a more compelling reason than the mere fact that things existed to want to *keep* seeing them. Otherwise you might end up as jaded as the Countess von Told, who in 1923 confided in an intertitle to her psychotherapist, Dr. Mabuse: "Everything that one can see from a car, or from a theater box, or from a window, is either disgusting or of little interest."

Some discipline was in order. The situation called for some-one to keep the spectators from looking away. Someone like an armed usher who would patrol the aisles of the theater and thwack any distracted patron. Grab his head if necessary; force the eyes back where they belonged, in the center of the screen. How could you make them pay attention?

It was necessary to instill a certain urgency. The watcher had to feel a nagging discomfort, an uneasy sense that if he failed to keep his eyes on the screen something unpleasant was going to happen to him. There was only one sure way to make the streets and telephones interesting again. The spectator had to be afraid of them.

The militant usher acquired a title: movie director. Direct-ing was a new human activity. The director regulated each nearly imperceptible shift and blink of the spectator's eye, each fugitive sigh of ennui or relief, every moment of sudden inexplicable dread. He laid down sluices to channel the flow of perception. He translated the nervous system into a gridwork of ornamental patterns, visual cadences to which total stran-gers would respond in almost identical fashion. The task was scientific.

I T W A S A question of narrowing the range of choice, to minimize both depth and periphery so that there could be no escape from the enclosed surface. Not surprising, then, that a student of architecture should so concisely and unerringly define the task at hand. The destiny of Dr. Mabuse's silent puppeteer, Fritz Lang, was to be nothing more or less than a movie director: as if he had been born to give the term a definition. He went about his job with the cool punctiliousness of the deeply obsessed.

It was almost by accident that the shots he constructed—with such relentless care that the actors and technicians were made to stay up for hours, until dawn if necessary, to make the thing come out exactly as specified—that these shots when placed side by side became a visual thesaurus of modern objects in space. It was like another splendid German invention, the Duden pictorial dictionaries which told you the name of every common object. In Lang's dictionary, however, every object had the same name: anxiety.

The inhabited areas—framed by strategically positioned pieces of furniture, objets d'art, mirrors, paintings—were shown to consist of nothing. Existence could be defined as what was demarcated by walls, from the walls of financial markets and opium dens to the wall of the horizon line, the wall of the sky, the wall of the eye. The people inside the rooms were instances of the effects of pressure. They moved with the deliberate slowness of underwater explorers, and their speech, while respecting the norms of casual banality, betrayed an unnatural hollowness, as if the unseen Doktor had subjected them to one of his hypnotic experiments.

Indeed, like his hypnotic master criminal, the director was a kind of doctor, paying close attention to the pulse and heart-beat of the viewer, who might as well, after all, have been strapped into the seat from which he watched a succession of plagues, suicides, shipwrecks, and ghostly visitations. Looking at the middle of the screen, he watched actors stare at him.

The rooms and streets slotted into each other like the com-partments of an immense prison. The camera studied the working of machines: conveyor belts, explosive devices, gam-bling wheels, instruments of torture. The nightclubs were ma-chines for channeling desire, running as smoothly and imper-sonally as the limousine fleets of the secret agents.

LANG PLANNED EVERY element—angles, movements, rhythms—in advance. The filming merely processed some-thing that already existed in his head. Lang used actors as if they were props, and got some of his best effects from inex-pressive performers like Louis Hayward (*House by the River*) and Dana Andrews (*Beyond a Reasonable Doubt*). As a child he played with toy theaters, staging "real fairy-tale shows, with changing sets," and in his movies he made a miniature world inhabited by actual people. He peered, as through a peephole, into a universe of discrete objects, where gestures and even feelings were apprehended as *things*.

He said that he felt a "curious, almost somnambulant cer-tainty" about how the images should look. When he worked he felt "almost as if I were sleepwalking." He would read the script and then close his eyes, sink into a sort of trance, and allow images to well up. In this way he "saw" the film with his inner eye, as if its finished form already existed within him.

And so he became himself a Fritz Lang movie: a film director, reading a lurid, melodramatic scenario, falls into a hypnotic state in which he receives commands from an unknown source; on waking he proceeds to carry them out with compulsive precision.

It was the world where the cake was a bomb and the doorbell was an eye. The vacant apartment exploded. The Nazi agent was the author of *The Psychoanalysis of Nazidom*. The betrayed artist painted the toenails of the woman he was going to murder, the woman who lay on the bed surrounded by mirrors. The things were inescapable: clocks, keys, doors, windows. Beams of light pinpointed them. Close-ups isolated their identity as if the world could be broken into interlocking pieces.

The screen was a map where you saw the people being trapped, ambushed, forced into hiding. The hero was held within a cave, a basement filling with water, a room whose walls closed in. It was a mechanism of pure instrumentality, devoid of interior life. The wife in *Secret Beyond the Door* knew that she was to be killed and she almost didn't care. "Can one kill by purposely denying someone love? By taking away the desire to live?" It might have been an experiment in which despair was systematically induced in laboratory animals.

The people were creatures of a frame, shadows cast against a screen. They spied on each other and duplicated each other's images, while the most powerful among them hoarded vast image banks through which they controlled reality. Everywhere the machinery of communication was deployed: the telephone, the television screen, the framed photograph, the tabloid headline. Trapped in the visible, the people looked at each other or looked away from each other. Glances were enclosures mirrored by labyrinthine streets and offices and caves and prisons.

His movies repeatedly enacted the same events, just as the obsessed criminals and victims of mind control who inhabited them had to perform the same actions over and over. The Chase In The Tunnel or The Seance At Which Murder Is Committed or The Flood In The Labyrinth: it didn't matter which. None could ever end or lead to anything further. They just recurred. Images could offer no release from images. The camera prowled through cell after cell and found no chinks. The material world—that hermetic interior—was bound seamlessly together, with just enough air to keep its inmates alive.

He did not so much make great films as make the same great film over and over. By the curious stasis and impersonality of his way of staging things, Fritz Lang embodied a stubbornness and durability, a durability beyond death like the boat-borne corpse of Stewart Granger in *Moonfleet* framed against a stony sea. In 1960 he could reiterate the compositions of 1919, and on leaving Germany could bleach out the remnants of Max Reinhardt and Arnold Böcklin and substitute stripped-down American ingredients: burnt-out ex-cons, gum-chewing steno girls, psycho killers reared on the comics, Spencer Tracy and Joan Bennett and Gloria Grahame, and Glenn Ford pretending to be (as the director confided to an interviewer) "Li'l Abner coming back from Korea—100 percent red-blooded American with very natural sex feelings (if such a thing exists)." The essence of the imperial architectonics of *Siegfried* and *Metropolis* was somehow reconstituted with cheap sets representing bars, diners, and police stations.

All that remained in the end was an unyielding tightness, a sharp focus with nothing left to focus on but the rote performances of zombie actors trapped in the screenplays of *Beyond a Reasonable Doubt* and *The Tiger of Eschnapur*. The world might change, but the camera—impersonal and soulless, the prisoner of its own mechanism—could finally only say one thing. It told what a camera was.

THE FILM WAS there to embody the worldview of its creator, "worldview" being definable as a personal philosophy bounded by barbed wire, broken glass, and trained attack dogs. An auteur like Hitchcock was an interior decorator using his fetishes for furniture. From his grid of relentless tracking shots and claustrophobic cross-cutting he rigorously excluded any item with which he was not obsessed. In Fritz Lang's early movies you found not Germany but what he had substituted for Germany. John Ford constructed a scale model containing all he wished to preserve of civilization—a portable world in which John Wayne and Ward Bond could swap drinks and war stories until the end of time—like a ship in a bottle perched among the charts and medals and pipes on the desk of a dying admiral.

The idea of cinematic authorship was not simply a tribute to merit and craftsmanship but an expression of faith: that the clouds or the tree acquired meaning because someone had put a frame around them. An author was an organizing principle. A movie looked different if you thought somebody directed it, just as the world looked different if you thought God planned it. The arbitrary became intentional. Fritz Lang meant for the cheap lamp to fill the upper left-hand corner of the screen. The angle at which the B-girl lit her cigarette was in accordance with his mysterious inexorable will. The very poverty of the sets and inexpressiveness of the acting manifested an invisible desire.

The movie took on the character of its maker as a party did of its host. Even if you didn't talk to him you could get an idea of what he was about from the furniture and the paintings and the music tape, not to mention the sort of people he invited. If you hung out at John Ford's place you could expect Irish whiskey, sentimental music, and an amiable fistfight on the porch. At von Sternberg's the air would reek of incense and opium, time would appear to slow down, and the host would be too preoccupied with adjusting the lights around Marlene Dietrich to pay much attention to his other guests. Von Stroheim had a more ruthless approach: you were simply not allowed to leave until you had seen all the rooms, studied everyone who was in them, proved that you had fully savored the oppressive weight of the structures they were caught in. The host came close to being an aggressor: "It's my party and I get to determine what's real!"

To the extent that you were aware of the director's presence, you became him. You wore his eyes like a pair of trick glasses turning everything you looked at into a military parade (John Ford), a masked ball (Max Ophuls), a series of medieval tableaux (Sergei Eisenstein), a blank-verse melodrama enacted by shadows (Orson Welles), or a fever dream in which you giggled as you watched your worst fears materialize (Luis Buñuel).

You inhabited the trajectory of the director's glance, the rhythm of his breathing. The whole nervous system joined in. Watching a Jean Renoir movie the body was relaxed, the eye ranging casually over its surroundings; with Robert Bresson, the body dropped away altogether except for the eye fixated on an apparently random detail until the hand or the donkey's foreleg became the universe.

If you watched the movie enough times you ended up feeling as if you had directed it, had conceived it; you could almost remember the dream in which you had glimpsed the germ of the idea for it. There could be but one volition; you identified yourself absolutely with the will that decreed how slowly the door would open or how long the camera would linger over the waving branches. Properly speaking, to perceive was simply to tune in to the frequency of that volition. You became the hum.

But this intimacy between viewer and director had strict limits. You never saw him, never heard his voice. You knew only that you were walking in his territory. Like an unseen landowner—like the cloistered Beast through whose endless empty rooms Beauty wandered amazed—he seemed to hover among the walks and shrubs and ponds of an otherwise deserted estate. If you wanted to go further—seek an audience with him, ask him what he really intended, demand an answer to whatever disturbance his landscaping had set in motion—he would reply only with the sign with which Orson Welles sealed his own definitive exercise in authorship, in the last frame of *Citizen Kane:* NO TRESPASSING.

In truth the director was a phantom. He haunted a house he had himself constructed—even if it was only a dollhouse. He came back again and again to his miniature world, his lagoon, his police station, his mist-hidden Himalayan enclave: those imaginary landscapes in which, alone among mortals, he was privileged to bury himself alive. By devoting his life to that illusion, the director was empowered to make the rest of humanity the spectators of his dream.

the souk of knowledge and the wide open spaces

—**B**ut what exactly have you taught us, Herr Doktor Lang?

All those revelations had clearly been some kind of learning experience, but what had been transmitted? The movies were full of things almost impossible to forget—names, faces, plots, lines of dialogue—but curiously devoid of anything like hard information. What you learned were useless things: the lyrics to "Lydia the Tattooed Lady," the names of all seven dwarfs or of all seven stars of *The Magnificent Seven* (with extra points for remembering Brad Dexter), who really killed Shawn Regan in *The Big Sleep* or who really got killed instead of Laura in *Laura,* how to distinguish Van Heflin from Van Johnson.

Indeed, the directors who made the most indelible marks on memory—Alfred Hitchcock, John Ford, Fritz Lang—were those who knew best how to exclude all information except the tiny amount required to give their dream narratives minimal coherence. Anything else would be a distraction, an intolerable trespass into the director's private world. The early film directors grew up in a world of books whose authors—Shakespeare, Dickens, Balzac—were revered for how much they managed to include. The cinematic sublime, by contrast, was founded on the art of omission. The film artist was judged by how much he could keep out, by the decisiveness with which he guarded the borders of his frame against invasion by the populous messiness outside the gates.

The language of which Lang and Hitchcock were the most rigorous masters had an infinite number of words (that is, people, places, objects) but hardly any meanings—a mere handful, ceaselessly redistributed. But the units of significance, however few, had an uncanny durability. Chase movies like *The Escaped Lunatic* (1903) simply continued from decade to decade, picking up slightly more elaborate trappings along the way. Instead of a sausage it was a missile they were after, and instead of proceeding on foot they used sonar. The native witch doctor from a 1919 German serial turned up with hardly any visible change in a 1987 Hong Kong horror movie. The emergence of a new generation of spectators prompted not fresh material but a refurbishing of the old. With the same stunned delight, successive generations of moviemakers stumbled on the concept of the wheel.

As a result, what you accumulated, by dint of watching movies over a period of decades, was not a wide knowledge of other places and times but rather an alarming quantity of information about lack of information. Eventually whole libraries would be required to collate it all: books of lists, books of records, the clowns, the goddesses, the rebels, the all-time turkeys, encyclopedias of trivia, comprehensive filmographies of every major Eastern European filmmaker, recommended viewing for Catholic high schools with synopses and critical ratings, price guides to collectible lobby cards, the great movie bloopers, the most scandalous nude scenes, given names and birthstones of the stars, famous filmland slayings, immortal furniture designers of the studio era. Fact: *Mogambo* (1953) was the first Hollywood movie filmed on location in French Equatorial Africa. Fact: In *Riffraff* (1946), in a Panamanian nightclub, a trio led by Anne Jeffries sang, in the Andrews Sisters manner, a tune entitled "Money Is the Root of All Evil." Fact: Rod Cameron began his career as a stand-in for Fred MacMurray.

It was a medium you could inhabit, like the cops in *Contract on Cherry Street* (1977) who conducted a movie trivia quiz over their radios until Harry Guardino snorted: "I don't have time to sit around asking why Humphrey Bogart picked up J. Carrol Naish in the desert in *Sahara* or why Conrad Veidt fell in love with Greta Garbo!" But you, who weren't a cop with a killer to catch, did have time.

THE BODY OF knowledge that drifted to you like flotsam from a wrecked caravel proved as insubstantial as the knowledge that characters in movies were supposed to possess: the mastery of fake tribal languages and ersatz native customs, the South Seas cosmologies of *Cobra Woman* and *Pearl of the South Pacific,* the thick and dangerous books of necromantic lore that

Dana Andrews puzzled over in *Curse of the Demon*. The routes that led to hidden valleys, lost islands, the ruins of alien civilizations: maps that crumbled on waking. There was no secret that had not been revealed; you had heard the incantation, you had seen the monster, you had survived the end of the world, and all without retaining a thing.

The most powerful influence was exerted at the peripheries, where the stray bits of pseudo-information tended to crop up. Sheer filler: the layout of rubber plantations in Malaya, how to suck venom out of snakebites, the irrevocable link between Russian peasants and balalaikas, the pinup inevitably found in at least one locker on every submarine, an Apache scout reading sign in a bleached arroyo ("Three men camp here two days gone"), bloodhounds losing the trail of the hunted when they come to a stream, the ability of a chased man to lose his pursuers by ducking into an alleyway or around a corner, the fine points of Coptic architecture laid out by Robert Taylor in *Valley of the Kings* or the crux of the jury system driven home by Henry Fonda in *Twelve Angry Men*, Shirley Yamaguchi in *House of Bamboo* explaining to Robert Stack why Japanese girls think eyebrows are sexy, secrets of marksmanship, Jesus healing lepers, how gangsters set themselves up business, come-on lines that dames go for.

You traced the history of all wars and revolutions, mastering the equivalences by which a Norman equaled a cattle baron and a Saxon a sheep farmer, a French aristocrat of the *ancien régime* equaled a Chinese warlord of the 1930s and a Mexican peon of the revolutionary era equaled a Vietnamese rice farmer determined to resist Communist takeover, Sir Francis Drake fought fascism on the high seas and Osceola's sincere plea for Seminole rights was undermined by the hidden radical agenda of tribal extremists.

The information sank in deepest if you knew nothing of Malaya and then saw *The Letter:* the empty file in the mind labeled "Malaya" all of a sudden had something to put in it. Even if you suspected or knew outright that the information was false, it was still something to hold on to, concrete and memorable. People who grew up watching *Shanghai Express* and *The Bitter Tea of General Yen* and *The General Died at Dawn, The Good Earth* and *Dragon Seed, The Left Hand of God* and *Soldier of Fortune* and *The Inn of the Sixth Happiness, 55 Days at Peking* and *The Sand Pebbles* and *Seven Women* ended up knowing a great deal more about "common misconceptions concerning China" than they ever would about China.

They learned some philosophy too. There were so many moments when people said unarguable things. "The only law that's worth a hang is the law of human nature," said Gene Lockhart in *Billy the Kid* in 1941. "It's strange how a man will cling to the earth when he feels he isn't going to see it again," said Spencer Tracy in *Bad Day at Black Rock* in 1955. "Only God has the right to play God," said John McIntire in *Two Rode Together* in 1961. It didn't matter what it meant, the cadence just felt right.

THE WESTERN, FOR example, derived its strength from the reiteration of what was already self-evident. "Sooner or later Diablito had to be stopped": that much had been demonstrated. The whole world was in on the lesson. Twenty million heads nodded in recognition of the moment when the reluctant gunman must finally draw. What, after all, did Josef Stalin and Douglas MacArthur, Ludwig Wittgenstein and Sherwood Anderson, Jorge Luis Borges and Akira Kurosawa have in common if not a love for cowboy pictures? They were basic cultural wallpaper offering the simplest of simple pleasures: a fistfight on the roof of a stagecoach, a body falling out a window, a man drinking from a river, a horse crossing a plain at full gallop, a hero allowing himself to surrender to pent-up rage.

The western became the genre of genres because it was most obviously the common property of the emerging global communications tribe. A new civilization, born of technology and advertising and intervals of military occupation, scavenged its myths as it went along. It found lariats and six-shooters in its path and scooped them up as it would later scoop up flying saucers and motorcycle gangs. The genre most widely diffused, most easily reduced to a simplistic common denominator, would be defined almost paradoxically as the "king" of genres: a kingship signifying not elitist exclusiveness but universal reach, penetrating the most isolated and primitive settlements.

Nowhere—not in Lapland or Fiji or the remotest estuaries of the Indian Ocean—was Hopalong Cassidy a stranger. *Shane* was as much a Japanese movie as it was American, *Django* as much a Jamaican movie as it was Italian. The nineteenth-century Teutonic idealism of Karl May—Germany's answer to James Fenimore Cooper—attained worldwide distribution in *Rampage at Apache Wells* (1966), which would turn up dubbed and cleansed of its national origin on American television and hardly anyone would notice the difference. The true history of the western would have to remember the childlike pulp novelist in Renoir's *Le Crime de Monsieur Lange* (1935), exulting in his fantasies of Arizona Jim, or Anna Magnani in Visconti's *Bellissima* (1951), watching *Red River* in a Roman slum and becoming jubilant over a scene of cattle wading through a river: "Look! The cows are all getting wet! It's marvelous!"

Westerns were reliable, minimal, direct, mindless, a series of clear actions occurring in an empty world where there was, over the long haul, nothing to worry about. Indians, outlaws, rustlers, and crooked railroad men emerged out of nowhere and were duly erased. A cowboy picture was an equation each of whose elements equaled zero, a drug that worked anywhere, an antidote to complexity like the cowboy himself, who sauntered into a disorderly town and made everything simple just by standing at the bar: "Tex McCloud. That's a nice name. I like it."

In like fashion a 1958 movie like *Man of the West* exerted emotional power simply by being there, by displaying its monolithic title on the marquee, by starring an aging Gary Cooper whose face belonged, according to Jean-Luc Godard, to "the mineral kingdom." Having maintained its primal repertoire of images and devices with less visible change than anything else, the western was symbolic home, a last living link with the primordial precinematic world. If the neighborhood movie theater was a secular church, the western was its liturgy.

THE WESTERN MOVIES were the most obtrusive feature of a huge stretch of territory encompassing battle sites, ghost towns, and federally protected rock formations—tourist attractions ranging from Walt Disney's Frontierland to woebegone theme parks like New Jersey's Wild West City, where decades later you could still see the marshal confront the outlaws on Main Street at high noon—plastic figurines of cowboys and Indians, toy six-guns, tom-toms, war bonnets—Vaughn Monroe singing "Ghost Riders in the Sky." The piling up of fantasies in the cultural compost gave westerns whatever authenticity they possessed: Buffalo Bill dime novels, the lyrics of "Goodbye Old Paint" and "Streets of Laredo," the paintings of Remington and Russell, Owen Wister's Virginian, Zane Grey's Lassiter, Clarence Mulford's Hopalong Cassidy, the radio exploits of the Lone Ranger.

There had to be something real at the bottom of all that. How else could it have stayed around so long? It was a world you could taste and smell, of skillets, stirrups, cattle tracks, dry boulders, sagebrush, leather. Something about the minutiae of horses or firearms or wagon wheels anchored you to the world. That aura of realness was the product you needed, the imaginary physicality of an imaginary history. Not that westerns were indifferent to history; on the contrary, they were excited by it, and by the pretense that they had some connection to it. Its artifacts, from watch fobs to Winchesters, provided fetishistic embellishment for narratives that otherwise existed completely outside of history.

From time to time, fresh infusions of the real helped spice the fantasy. For one generation, authenticity had been represented by the folksy humor of Gabby Hayes or Smiley Burnette, for another by the luxurious pseudo-historicism of romantic pageants like *Jesse James* (1939) and *They Died with Their Boots On* (1941). The innovative psychosexual furies of *Duel in the Sun* (1947) and *Pursued* (1947) gave way to the self-congratulatory tolerance of *Broken Arrow* (1951) and the civic allegorizing of *High Noon* (1952). By the late fifties, the western tended to demonstrate its maturity by introducing themes of sexual violence (*Jubal, The Bravados, Man of the West, Last Train from Gun Hill*) and racial conflict (*Trooper Hook, Flaming Star, Sergeant Rutledge, The Unforgiven*).

The filmmakers went marching forward into the past. They edged ever closer to its reality until, as they came up against a hitherto invisible limit, the whole thing smashed to pieces. The spectacle of that destruction provided the most beautiful fireworks of an era: the slow-motion exploding blood bags of Sam Peckinpah and the violent calligraphic operas of Sergio Leone. Feeding on an always implicit threat of random violence—on an increasingly restless urge to move, to make a noise, to smash something—the genre lurched like a half-drunk gunslinger toward its apocalypse.

A profound underlying boredom was the emotional basis of westerns. They were basically about killing time. They were what there was to do in town, in America, year after year. The boy who grew up in a Texas town remembered it as the place where he saw *3:10 to Yuma* and *Last Train from Gun Hill* and *The Badlanders* and *The Bravados.* At times it seemed even to him that he didn't really come from a Texas town, he came from *The Man from Texas,* he came from *Terror in a Texas Town* just like everybody else.

Westerns invented almost nothing. Their effectiveness lay precisely in the flatness and exhaustion with which they reenacted the tension and dread that defined a universal male culture of playgrounds, locker rooms, army barracks, and prison yards.

THE OPENNESS OF the wide open spaces served as a means of protection. The western landscape was a place where the hero could get lost and hide out forever from everything. The childish perception of landscape was formerly colored, to a degree that would later become difficult to imagine, by the western's uses for forest and gully and butte. Cowboy pictures taught what space was for. Small-scale pictures like *The Naked Spur* and *Ride Lonesome* became huge by playing off the tiny actors against their huge surroundings: the isolated human figures served as devices for measuring rock spurs and crevices and abysses.

The vistas, whether of keelboats going up the Missouri (*The Big Sky*) or of canoes skirting the Everglades (*Distant Drums*), were often reason enough to watch. Yet for the most part western movies had little real use for wilderness or exploration. They never went deep enough or lingered long enough, not even John Ford's movies. They were always in too much of a hurry to get back to the closed human worlds of the fort, the town, the mining camp, the stagecoach station.

Finally they were not so much epics as studies in claustrophobia and repetition, offering not wide open spaces but dead ends, the canyons and defiles of ambush, the mesa beyond which there's nowhere else to hide, the alleys and stables where men on the run are cornered. "They've got this whole town boxed up." The western's formal problem was not to open up space—it started with open space—but to shut it down, to make it ever tighter and narrower. The underlying menace of westerns was clarified belatedly in the title of a 1970s horror movie: *The Hills Have Eyes,* whether they belonged to cattle rustlers or thirst-crazed army deserters dragging a load of gold bullion through Death Valley or a Comanche raiding party. "When you can't see 'em, they're lookin' at you" (*Run of the Arrow*).

The way the figures were hemmed in by their landscape mirrored the way they were caught within their rather limited behavioral rules. There were no corners to hide in, no room to back up: the aesthetic of the prison yard again. It was a system of traps where there was really only one plot: the man whose hand was forced, who was shoved and shoved until he had to shoot to kill. The western hero had no freedom. He forever had to be watching his back and keeping an eye on the rimline.

The landscape was a book containing ominous coded messages: embers, broken twigs, suspicious bird calls. The country where masked men rode was itself a mask. Or it was a painted face: the face of the Indian suddenly looming up out of the underbrush, a favorite shot in the fifties, particularly suited for 3-D. As emblems of a terror nearly indistinguishable from the natural world, Indians served as supremely efficacious decorative elements. So successfully were they camouflaged by the land that they virtually were the land, as if the phrase "Seminole country" implied a complicity between landscape and savage. Yet the fear was bound up with the spectator's pleasure, with the sensory thrill of that blend of war paint as fright mask and incessant drumming: *Distant Drums, Apache Drums, Yaqui Drums, A Thunder of Drums, Drum Beat.*

IF INDIAN WARS represented a struggle against nature, the problems of the new settlements revolved around the unnatural, the deformed, the misbegotten. Sick and violent men caused trouble and had to be put down. "A single rotten apple spoils the barrel"—*Bend of the River*. The hero was often little more than a blunt object for a range of colorful evil to bump up against. The ostensible moral seriousness of "adult" fifties westerns like *High Noon, The Gunfighter, 3:10 to Yuma,* and *The Bravados* was consistently undercut by their fascination with a fauna of male evil and dysfunction: Robert Ryan, Ernest Borgnine, Jack Elam, Neville Brand, Charles McGraw, Lee Van Cleef, Leo Gordon, Ray Teal, Earl Holliman, Lee Marvin, Charles Bronson. (Marvin and Bronson were constant presences throughout the fifties and sixties before finally becoming stars, as if to acknowledge belatedly the scarred and downbeat level of reality they represented.)

The title *Garden of Evil* appropriately tagged the western's catalogue of the many ways in which males could fail to measure up: spineless gamblers, equivocating lawyers, businessmen huffing and puffing in the face of Indian trouble, young hotshots too quick on the trigger, reservation agents conducting a black-market trade in rifles and whiskey, dying cavalry commanders blinded by pride, alcoholic mutineers, desperadoes with a mean streak liberated by the absence of law. Cowardice, cruelty, fanaticism, petty thievery, just plain goofing off: these were the raw materials out of which a commander (Gregory Peck in *Only the Valiant* or Randolph Scott in *Seventh Cavalry*) had to make a functioning unit.

The losers finally broke out and took over in the era of the "dirty" western: *Rio Conchos* (1964), *The Professionals* (1966), *The Wild Bunch* (1969), *Dirty Little Billy* (1972), and the more than three hundred spaghetti westerns produced between 1963 and 1969. For Americans, to gaze into the distorting mirrors of *Django* and *Sabata*—a man dragging a coffin through mud, a priest forced to eat his own ear—was to find a more congenially nasty image than what had been filtered through the pieties of *Gunsmoke* and *Bonanza:* a landscape of tin shacks and mud puddles, a supporting cast of whores and hired assassins, and an unhypocritical defense of eye-gouging and below-the-belt punches, served up by frankly self-serving, lecherous heroes who (unlike James Stewart in *The Naked Spur* or Gregory Peck in *The Bravados*) positively relished the opportunity for revenge.

The western hero, once an Arthurian knight of the plains, ended up more closely resembling a cocaine dealer in cowboy drag. And that transition too was added to your knowledge: how long it took for an image to erode, and what it looked like at each stage of the process. You measured your own duration against the half-life of icons.

So film history charted the evolution of tiny mutations, as if everybody set out to make exactly the same movie—like monks copying out the writings of Origen and Athanasius—and failed in revealing ways. The failed imitation then became someone else's original.

If practically all your knowledge came from movies, the same went—in spades—for the people who made them. You went to the movies to encounter a world that moviemakers were far too busy even to see. It crept in as if by accident, with some help from location scouts. The paint-by-numbers intrigue of *Shaft in Africa* found itself unexpectedly invaded by an actual Ethiopian airport. The thief of Bagdad wandered in the Grand Canyon. The two-headed grotesqueries of a horror movie called *The Manster* were intercut with certifiably genuine scenes of Japanese nightclubs and hot springs resorts.

These coalescing fragments might have been struggling to regain a lost oneness. Movies were born universal, after all. In the years immediately following their invention the same print could travel from country to country without alteration: a raw inscription legible anywhere. Slip in different intertitles and a German monster was an American monster. Only gradually did the globe split into separate parallel zones, a process speeded up by the divisive introduction of talking pictures. These parallel universes had names like Italy, Mexico, Japan, Egypt, India, the Soviet Union; but their inhabitants sensed obscurely that on a deeper level they were common citizens of Movieland.

For a hundred years humans had been communicating obliquely by absorbing the crisscrossing reflections that bounced from one movie to another, one nation to another. In 1933 a Trinidad calypso song summarized the plots of *International House* and *We're Not Dressing.* Mexican movies turned up in China, Indian movies in Russia, Japanese movies in France, American movies in Germany. America, source of so many of the images, was perhaps least aware of all the borrowings and mutations: but then Hollywood was itself a collage, importing not movies but moviemakers and actors, internalizing Germany as Marlene Dietrich, France as Charles Boyer, Hungary as Peter Lorre.

The sharpest separation occurred at mid-century, with the world divided into zones of cinematic exclusion, and the fascist countries busily developing alternative Hollywoods. Instead of *Young Mr. Lincoln* or *Drums Along the Mohawk,* Italian audiences were watching sagas of Italy's wars of liberation in Africa: *Bronze Sentries, The White Squadron, The Pilot Luciano Serra.* (Outside the theater they could whistle current hits like "Tripoli, Beautiful Land of Love" and "The Caravans of the Tigrai Are Marching On.") Meanwhile, in Southeast Asia, the occupying Japanese had blocked the further distribution of the popular American movies and set about instilling a taste for such contemporary Japanese productions as *Fifth Column Fear, Flower of Patriotism, Endless Advance,* and *Toward the Decisive Battle in the Sky.*

Forty years later, Javanese moviegoers could still hum the theme from *Flower of Patriotism,* the story of a military nurse and her devotion to duty. The war of movies pitted identical images against each other: military nurses displayed the same spirit of self-sacrifice in Japan's *Flower of Patriotism,* Italy's *The White Ship,* and America's *So Proudly We Hail!* The John Wayne vehicle *Back to Bataan* had its reverse image in *Fire on That Flag!,* a Japanese movie, made in the Philippines in 1944, which according to an archivist emphasized "the brutality of the U.S. Army contrasted with the humanity of the Japanese Army."

Enemy movies: the idea was entrancing, as if to watch them would be to peer into closed worlds you were never intended to see. Clearly legible in the captured footage—*Paracelsus* or *The Crown of Iron* or *The White Ship* or *The Magic Sword*—were glimpses of foreign rituals, initiations into brotherhoods of vengeance, implications of voluntary mass suicide. Pieces of hieratically choreographed Japanese sword fights would be excised and spliced into a documentary called *Know Your Enemy:* the formality of the gestures and the forbidding elegance of the camera movements combined to create an impression of creatures from another planet practicing some unspeakably violent ceremony.

Yet on closer examination they were more similar than different. There must once have been real differences between places, but by the 1940s everybody was living in some variant of Hollywood. The Nazi propaganda movies horrified not because they were monstrously alien but because they were written in an intimately familiar language of visual storytelling, the language of John Ford and Frank Capra.

Even in what seemed a genuinely hermetic world you found your own, as you came out on the far side of otherness into the camera movements of Mizoguchi's *The Loyal 47 Ronin*. Somehow Mizoguchi was doing the same kind of thing with tracking shots and deep focus that Welles and Hitchcock were working with over in their corner, as if all the movie directors in the world enjoyed a telepathic communion transcending political lines. A lens is a lens. The universality of technology annulled the momentary oddness of localized dialogue: "We are grateful for being ordered to disembowel ourselves." "It seems that they all died without being disgraceful."

Paramount among the fruits of victory for American filmmakers was the return of international distribution. After the war the Japanese were entranced by American movies. Akira Kurosawa, whose *Sanshiro Sugata* (1943) had been widely distributed to Japanese-occupied countries as an object lesson in the self-discipline of the judo spirit, was by 1949 making an impeccable film noir: *Stray Dog,* transplanting Dore Schary's documentary style to the dance halls and shanty towns of Tokyo's back streets. Yukio Mishima's favorite actress was

Ann Blyth. The young Japanese men couldn't get enough of cowboy pictures, especially *Shane.* A man speaking of his student days remembered how he would play Ferde Grofe's *Grand Canyon Suite* on his record player and lie back with his eyes closed thinking of images from *Shane.*

The other movie the postwar kids all remembered was Kurosawa's *Seven Samurai,* because the strength of it, and the fact that it was Japanese, made it clear that the war was finally truly over. Ten years the later the Americans would remake it as *The Magnificent Seven,* and from that one the Italians would get most of the clichés for their own hybrid, just as Sergio Leone would lift the scenario of *A Fistful of Dollars* from Kurosawa's *Yojimbo* (itself derived from the fiction of Dashiell Hammett), before Sam Peckinpah could set about doing his own mix of elements from the Japanese swordsman pictures, as if he had stored up the memory of each rhapsodic slow-motion slashing and balletic eruption of blood.

While the Japanese were inventing America, the Americans were inventing Japan in *House of Bamboo* (1955), *Sayonara* (1957), *Escapade in Japan* (1957), *Stopover Tokyo* (1957), and *The Geisha Boy* (1958). Geishas, orphans, and the Great Buddha at Kamakura featured prominently, as the apparently impervious ancient culture was subjected to the archetypally American onslaughts of Robert Ryan, Marlon Brando, Red Buttons, and Jerry Lewis: a battle of styles. The Americans went so far as to impersonate the Japanese, an imposition only a conqueror would venture, from Marlon Brando in *The Teahouse of the August Moon* (1956) to Mickey Rooney in *Breakfast at Tiffany's* (1961)—not to mention Shirley MacLaine *pretending* to be Japanese in *My Geisha* (1962), so successfully that her own husband (Yves Montand, *pretending* to be a veritable Hollywood star rather than a rejected foreign transplant) didn't catch on.

The exchange became more complex with Toshiro Mifune wandering with a sword around the Old West in *Red Sun* (1971), Robert Mitchum losing a finger to the Japanese gangsters' pitiless code of loyalty in *The Yakuza* (1975), and Steven Spielberg transforming the Pacific war into an occasion for good-natured international comedy in *1941* (1979). On the Japanese side, Hollywood plots and images were spliced and recombined in movies that looked the same but felt just that little inexplicable bit different, like the horror movie *Vampire Doll,* which replicated bits of *Rosemary's Baby* and *Dark Shadows* and set them to work in a context incomprehensible to an American viewer.

VAMPIRE DOLL DIDN'T travel so well, and perhaps the Japanese were immune to Britain's "Carry On" movies. Hindi musicals, Arabic melodramas, arty French horror porno, and Hong Kong sex comedies did not cross over into "worldwide" outside their own language groups. But the industrialized democracies could hardly complain, seeing how much else they got: horror movies from England's Hammer films, Mexican vampires, a smattering of Japanese swordsmen and a flood of Chinese kickboxers, Russian science fiction, Swedish soft-core, American blaxploitation.

That was only a beginning. It was just getting under way, like the process by which bits and pieces of Frankish and Burgundian and Langue d'Oc gradually turned into French, and

Tunisian beachfront hotels gradually turned into Miami, Toulouse turned into Dakar, Dakar turned into Los Angeles. Day and night the images were being reprocessed. Video made it happen all that much faster. Somewhere out there in the so-called Third World the images were going through yet other cycles which would in due time become apparent, as the spiritual heirs of *The Big Boss* or *Saturday Night Fever* or *RoboCop 2* emerged from some unlikely coral reef or mountain stronghold. In 1968 Jimmy Cliff and his pals watched the spaghetti western *Django* in a Kingston fleapit before emerging to act it out. The woman who lived in Ayacucho before the Shining Path guerrillas got up to full steam said she knew there was going to be trouble, the way the young men did nothing but ride around on their Hondas and watch those kung fu movies.

Somewhere the ragged print of a Mexican wrestling movie, the sprocket holes nearly shot, is getting one more screening in an outpost too remote to have gotten hold of more recent product. It's the same one you saw on Channel Nine at three in the morning, and felt as if for once you were plugging into a genuinely international form of communication: a borderless flea market of used visions.

the italian system

You wandered in memory through a worldwide junk heap of images—like the makeshift souks of *Blade Runner* and *Mad Max Beyond Thunderdome*—trying to recall the big central display window that existed once, in the shiny world before the center failed. There had come an intermediary period full of signs and portents. The display began to wobble, as if there had all that time been only one light source and it was starting to flicker. Or as if a voice were going hoarse, the only voice in the entertainment world with enough authority to recite: "During the reign of Caesar Augustus, Herod the Great was ruler over all Judaea. And there came to him wise men . . ." In the last days of imperial Hollywood, the big show was the spectacle of the show's disappearance.

The Roman Empire photographed its own decay, as Alec Guinness morosely examined the entrails of sacrificed animals, Charlton Heston's corpse was propped up inside his armor to ride into battle against the Moors, and Steve McQueen died trying to hold at bay the inexorable energies of Chinese revolution. So many movies were about the aging and imminent death of their stars. The heroism of cowboys was transmuted into the heroism of the actors still just capable of playing them.

In the same spirit you were meant to admire the self-destructive extravagance with which the remnants of the studios squandered their resources on histories the audience no longer believed in (if indeed it had even heard of them). After another generation, the Roman Empire would exist only as a footnote to movie history: "Ancient political structure on which films such as *Spartacus* and *Ben-Hur* were based, noted for orgies, chariot races, and acid repartee enunciated by British actors."

It was an intolerably protracted farewell to the old money that had commanded legions of extras; that built three-dimensional sets the size of small cities and then burned them down; that when it clapped made all eyes swivel toward the marquees and billboards and magazine covers it monopolized. The pleasure of the late imperial spectacle was steeped in the cruelty of that slow death. You savored the gradual involuntary abdication as you had been taught to savor the death scenes of Garbo in *Camille* or the wounded GIs in *Battle Hymn*.

All signs spoke of the end: the atrophied camera movements, the crowds so huge they became undirectable and milled about listlessly, the lab effects that might once have passed unnoticed but became glaringly evident when blown up to the grandiose proportions of the 70-millimeter frame, the leaden pauses that existed only to emphasize the *duration* of the program, as if in those last desperate days mere length became a survival tactic. "Make it last forever, there may never be another one." *How the West Was Won, 55 Days at Peking, The Fall of the Roman Empire:* the hugeness of history established a scale which could then be applied indiscriminately to elephantine comedies (*It's a Mad, Mad, Mad, Mad World, The Great Race*), auto-race movies whose amplitude worked curiously against the grain of their high-speed spins and crack-ups (*Grand Prix*), musicals so disproportionate that they seemed to lose all relation to the human body (*Doctor Dolittle, Star!, Hello, Dolly!*). Bigness by now was destiny, or malediction. To expand uncontrollably was as malign a fate as to shrink.

The aging studio czars and their accountant successors couldn't control the scale of things anymore. A remorseless stiffening of reflexes had set in. The images were born old. Audiences woke as if from a long slumber to find themselves looking at a state-of-the-art wax museum, the Gimbel's window come to fitful life: a Grace Kelly look-alike with dyed hair lip-synched her dialogue against a slightly grainy rear projection representing New York's fashionable East 78th Street, to which the music of Neal Hefti or Frank de Vol tried desperately to lend animation. The crackle of sexual innuendo slowed to a blind glacial crunch. Where had the other spectators gone, the ones for whom these images had evidently been intended? What plague or systematic program of assassination had kept them from attending?

The latest sophisticated comedy looked like a promotional short for a hotel chain with empty rooms in every major capital. Indeed, Hollywood was going the way of the beloved old New Orleans hotel in *Hotel,* caught between buyout by money men who would trample its soul and the wrecker's ball that would obliterate it. In the last reel Rod Taylor (probably the lone heroic hotel manager in movie history) opted for the wrecker's ball, and then in proper sixties fashion set about getting stoned down in the bar where the last blast, the party at the end of the world, was just getting into gear. The drinks were on the house.

THE TROUBLE IN the empire was highlighted by the encounter, in Hollywood's shadow, with another Hollywood, its cheap twin. The Americans now *had* to make movies that were long and ponderous, as if to do anything less would be a surrender as abject as to withdraw from Southeast Asia. The resources had to be wasted to prove that they were still there to waste. But in Europe it was still possible to work with enough speed and violence and crudity to make movies suited to the world they were being shown in. They had sets and music too, and jazzy main title sequences, just like real movies: like a watch sold on the street corner that could almost pass for a Rolex if you didn't examine it too closely.

The European movies playing on Times Square in 1964 formed part of a multi-episode, multinational serial set in The City (a modular megalopolis of which Rome, Frankfurt, Cairo, and New Delhi were interchangeable subdivisions) with its computer networks, its hotel chains, its Möbius-strip highway systems, its canned music converting piazzas into wraparound amplifiers, its transnational corporations implementing mind control through synthetic drugs and programmed orgies.

Jets linked its scattered centers. Never had there had been so many shots of jets taking off, always accompanied by electric guitar music. A jet might take off in one movie and land in another. The deplaning passengers might even encounter some of the same actors, or at least actors who resembled them as uncannily as the androids that rogue masterminds were mass-producing in concealed laboratories scattered around the globe.

A common vocabulary had been uncovered, a glossary appropriate for any movie made outside the Iron Curtain, a set of cards that could be reshuffled to generate instant screenplay: airport, amnesia, assassination, atom bomb, blackmail, bondage, cavern, criminal gang, desert, drug hallucination, dual personality, explosion, fashion model, fire, impalement, insanity, jewelry, jungle, laboratory, lesbianism, luxury hotel, mutilation, narcotics, nightclub, nightmare, poison, police investigator, prostitute, psychiatrist, rape, religious cult, satanism, secret society, sequestered island, speedboat, strangulation, striptease, telepathy, telephone, tomb, torture.

Within this field of elements things were made to happen by manipulating the rules of fetishism—not changing them, just nudging them into unforeseen corners. It was a live-action encyclopedia, a zoo of captive gestures. Each imprisoned object exerted a familiar but somehow inexhaustible magnetism. This method of filmmaking might be called for the sake of convenience the Italian System.

All the movies ever made constituted a storehouse of images waiting to be appropriated and pasted into place:

Music Box (*The Criminal Life of Archibaldo de la Cruz, Two*

Rode Together, The Ghost, For a Few Dollars More). Childhood, the pain of memory. Sets off a magical or hypnotic process; summons the murderer to his task; restores identity to the amnesiac. Must be smashed or drowned. Its violent disappearance is equivalent to a spiritual liberation.

Madhouse (*The Cabinet of Dr. Caligari, Spellbound, Bedlam, Shock Corridor, Shock Treatment, House of Madness*). The world is a madhouse. The keeper is himself a madman. The inmate's delusion encrypts the solution to an actual crime.

Likewise: the mirror, the dark glasses, the ray that shrinks or makes invisible, the suitcase stuffed with dollars, the tunnel, the harem, the theatrical dressing room, the police station, the scalpel, the snapshot, the painting, the scarf, the glove, the hat, the window, the secluded cabin, the caged animal, the trapdoor (a thick round handle embedded in the floor), the woods (flight), the streetlamp (violence), rain, cyclone . . .

The letter being written, the letter being torn up or burned, the ring, the locket, the blow, the concealed glance of lust or adoration, the look of recognition, the grimace of hidden envy . . .

The skull, the abyss, the barred door. The tattoo. The scar, the mark of the branding iron.

THE ITALIAN SYSTEM, honorifically: because it was at Rome's Cinecittà studio, and subsequently at Rome's outposts in Spain and Yugoslavia (cut-rate outposts of an empire bought out by entrepreneurial barbarians from New Jersey and West Berlin), that the system was brought to its highest level of automatism. All pretense of telling a new story was abandoned in favor of luxuriating in the intimately predictable contours of the old story. It was a sort of unmasking, as if to say: Look how cheap it is, how hasty, how loud, how unoriginal. *È formidabile, no?*

Was it Hollywood's mirror, or had Hollywood itself all along been only a mirror of a lost European splendor that had secretly survived every catastrophe? Which was the authentic fake, the Ur-ersatz? Cinecittà was before Hollywood. It was what Hollywood had fed on. In the beginning—in the bright dawn that was April 1914—were the volcanoes and elephants and Carthaginian battles of Giovanni Pastrone's *Cabiria,* the virgins fed to the flaming maw of Moloch, the erotic soliloquies and operatic slow-motion death of Queen Sophonisba, the energetic exertions of the good-natured, simple-minded giant Maciste.

It was in *Cabiria* that D. W. Griffith found the germ of the idea for *Intolerance,* and if his inspiration hadn't been *Cabiria* it would have been *The Slave of Carthage* or *The Queen of Nineveh* or *The Virgin of Babylon* or *Fabiola* or *Herodias* or *Theodora.* From the beginning the Italians had recognized in film an opportunity to frame mute divas—Lyda Borelli, Pina Menichelli, Italia Manzini—against Mesopotamian wall hangings. They found their paradise early, and embellished it tirelessly with harps, tigers, fans, orchids, baths, patterned carpets, brooches, sandals, slaves, phalanxes, peacocks, gigantic stone idols, poisonous gardens. The images were visual incense: you inhaled them.

Here too was history, but a history that did what it was told, a sensual history freely adapting itself to the silks and fountains in the midst of which it had been resurrected. Beautiful ghosts were brought out to show off their costumes and perform their appointed turn: Nero, Messalina, Saint Sebastian, Faust, Socrates, Julius Caesar, Lucrezia Borgia, Saint Cecilia, and (for a parting burst of carnivalesque color) Ali Baba and Satan. The past was a festival where no desire was denied.

Cinecittà was then concurrent with Hollywood, competing with the relentless American marketing machine, cooperating with it (in a spirit of mutual mistrust) for the location sequences of the silent *Ben-Hur,* with Black shirt labor stooges stirring up trouble on the set while extras (who, desperate for cash, had lied about being able to swim) drowned to make possible the extraordinary naval battle. Mussolini banned *Ben-Hur* for local consumption anyway, once he found out that the Roman lost the chariot race. In the end it was determined that Italy could do without American movies, and the American market.

But Fascist cultural directives didn't constrict things all that much. In fact, they provided an ideal pretext for continuing to make movies about banquets, vengeance, and slaves, with emphasis added for the moment on the glories rather than the decadence of the Roman Empire. The nostalgia for world domination was transmuted into the creation of miniature worlds: the jungles and deserts of an imaginary Africa, the brocaded bedrooms of Renaissance princesses, and interiors sculpted out of gauze and rock candy to frame the operatic climaxes of *The Crown of Iron* and *Captain Tempest* and *An Adventure of Salvator Rosa.* Here no blow told, death was music, battle was decorative, and all endings were suffused with an exquisitely tearful happiness.

For a time, time froze. Out in the great world great things were done: heroic Phalangists defended Toledo against the Republican onslaught, saintly missionaries planted the seeds of faith in Libyan wastes, nurses tended the wounds of soldiers. As if to demonstrate what gestural code the recruits had been commanded to mime, *Tosca* and *Cavalleria Rusticana* and the life of Verdi came to lend their support. Those in the interior zone—shy, inarticulate young couples, stenographers, defense workers—could still find something to marvel at in the designs and protocols of a modern department store. It would provide the basis for a wistful, ultimately reassuring little comedy: *Their Day in the City*.

HAVING SURVIVED ALL that, Cinecittà began to look as if it would survive Hollywood as well. It had made itself the surrogate Hollywood, Hollywood's Hollywood, a low-cost recycling plant for every cast-off plot device and visual motif, not to mention every used-up actor and director: drunks, wilted starlets, aging cowboy actors, former colleagues of Griffith and Ince unemployable in the new Hollywood.

It took Italy to reinvent the faces of Rory Calhoun, Guy Madison, Reed Hadley, Brett Halsey, Ray Danton—certifiably American actors designed to impart authenticity to their surroundings—and to juxtapose their faded nobility with the fresher beauty of Genevieve Grad, Helga Line, Wandisa Guida, or Nadir Baltimor, under the imported directorial tutelage (filtered through some unimaginable fracas of multilingual interpretation) of Raoul Walsh, Irving Rapper, Hugo Fregonese, or Jacques Tourneur.

It was as close as movies got to a cultural lineage, this process of spirals within spirals by which you got the myth (the real, original Italian epics, *Cabiria* and *Quo Vadis* and *The Fall of Troy,* that took America by storm in 1914) and the myth of the myth (the improved and homogenized American epics, *Intolerance* and *Ben-Hur* and *The Queen of Sheba,* which in turn found their way back to Italian screens) and then, beyond computing, the myths of the myths of the myths, as each photographed the other's photographs: the Fascist historical epics with their perfect emulation of Hollywood gloss (*Scipio Africanus, The Crown of Iron*), the fifties Hollywood spectacles that took advantage of cheap Italian backdrops and extras (*Helen of Troy*) and the Italian spectacles that took advantage of Hollywood stars (Kirk Douglas in *Ulysses*), the even cheaper Italian imitations of those spectacles (*Hercules, Hercules Unchained, The Loves of Hercules*) that turned unemployed bodybuilders from Muscle Beach into authentic European stars and ultimately—by way of drive-ins and neighborhood chains—back into authentic American antistars, the first major figures in the impending anti-aesthetic with its cult of the bad.

The coilings became ever more inextricable: the art movie *La Dolce Vita* mythologized the sleazy underbelly of the Cinecittà world through the emblematic figures of Anita Ekberg and Lex Barker, the Hollywood movie *Two Weeks in Another Town* mythologized *La Dolce Vita* with Kirk Douglas and Edward G. Robinson masquerading as has-beens washed up in Rome, the horror queen Barbara Steele of *Black Sunday* and *Castle of Blood* turned up in Fellini's *8½,* and when Jean-Luc Godard made his solitary concession to narrative filmmaking (entitled, precisely, *Contempt*) it had to revolve around an

Italo-American remake of *The Odyssey* produced by Jack Palance and directed by Fritz Lang. (Lang had already made his Italian-style movie, not in Italy but in India, in German: a diptych divided into *The Tiger of Eschnapur* and *The Indian Tomb,* in which the director—scrupulously adhering to the 1921 scenario he was remaking—charted with hieratic precision the process by which a nearly expressionless German architect fell in love with a temple dancer incarnated by Debra Paget and had in consequence to do battle with rajahs and tigers and lepers.)

Two Weeks in Another Town caught the Italian method, in approximately the sense that one contracts a malady. This was entirely appropriate, since the movie's theme was the decline of Hollywood and the spiritual wreckage exposed in the process of that decline. It was as if M-G-M had decided to commit a peculiarly cinematic suicide by filming its own death. Director Vincente Minnelli and producer John Houseman incorporated ghostly references to their earlier collaboration *The Bad and the Beautiful,* just to twist the knife in the wound. They depicted the breakup of their world while remaining faithful until the last gasp to its forms and methods, displaying a loyalty as unwavering as that of disgraced samurai committing *seppuku.*

The bright, easily distinguishable modular units that made up *Two Weeks in Another Town* could serve as an internationally viable glossary of human feeling and knowledge circa 1962. Love: a couple walking at night holding hands against a background of Roman fountains, or lying on a beach sharing a bottle of red wine in a wicker wrapping. Debauchery: Kirk Douglas with his arms around three different women simultaneously, smashing a table, roaring with laughter. The male crisis of middle age: he looks at his hand shaking, or talks to a doctor in a room filled with leather-bound medical books.

George Hamilton means bisexuality, youthful weakness and uncertainty, complicated neuroses. Rome means comical waiters, hustling agents and producers, temperamental starlets, *La Dolce Vita*. Europe, more broadly, means *La Dolce Vita* (noise, orgies, international cast) plus *Bonjour Tristesse* (youthful perversity, jaded middle age) plus *Last Year at Marienbad* (elegant clothes, hieratically slow movements, inexplicable gaps and reversals in narrative continuity). Authenticity: Dahlia Lavi's neighborhood where ragged little boys play soccer in the street, poetic poverty, Neorealist movies from ten years earlier. Anger: Kirk Douglas driving his sports car at high speed toward a (rear-projected) wall. Spiritual rebirth: the car's impact is not fatal and Kirk Douglas is drenched by jets of water from the wreckage of a conveniently located fountain. The sober regrets of maturity—coinciding with the general sense that it is time for the movie to end—are represented by people saying goodbye at an airport in the morning.

They are saying goodbye to the place where they made an imaginary movie somehow more real than the one you just watched. On that edge of self-definition, it's as if a movie were trying to weasel its way out of its own existence—this isn't real, it's the *other* one inside this one that was real, the one you'll never see. The ultimate film festival would then have to consist of ghost movies: the low-budget *risorgimento* period piece that Edward G. Robinson almost finished shooting in *Two Weeks in Another Town*, Fritz Lang's *Odyssey*, the Crucifixion movie that Orson Welles was directing in Pasolini's *La Ricotta*, and the movie that (in Fellini's *Toby Dammit*) the alcoholic actor played by Terence Stamp had flown to Cinecittà to star in: the first Catholic western, "something between Dreyer and Pasolini with a touch of John Ford, of course."

THE SEDUCTIVE CHARM of the Italian fantasy epics, as they infiltrated unsuspecting neighborhoods all over the world, was the experience of watching a movie that was not a "real" movie but rather a movie of a movie, in the same way you might find yourself dreaming that you were dreaming. This was not *Ben-Hur,* it was a curious REM-state deformation of *Ben-Hur.*

For one long interval—the Age of Dress-Up—it was as if a relatively young child with a propensity for storytelling had been cajoled into spinning out a single open-ended tale, an adventure without beginning or end, while a team of screenwriters took notes. To the child's basic outline were added a few adult touches: literary references and a hint of decadent sexuality.

This was how it went. A group of beings who had come from the moon centuries earlier took up residence in a huge grotto. They were ruled by a tyrannical queen who secretly worshiped a fire-breathing mask hidden behind a curtain. She hypnotized everybody in sight, slipped sleeping potion in Hercules' goblet, and cleverly convinced the sacred oracle of the goddess to tell Ursus that Hercules was the one who sold his mother into slavery. A ceremony was to take place at the base of an idol. A pair of Kurdish wrestlers were brought out for entertainment. The queen's personal maid was accused of witchcraft in order that she might be spirited away to the dungeon. She was rescued by a man wearing a helmet in the shape of a wolf's head. Meanwhile the Greek hero was condemned to undergo what was termed "the truth test," which meant that he must engage in mortal combat with a giant gorilla. The conspirators were hiding out in the forest, getting ready to attack the city. Escaped slaves built a stockade. The queen kept going back to the curtain and making smoke come out of it. Maciste confronted the Echo-men, who destroyed people's minds by making loud sounds. It was at this point that the usurpers found themselves surrounded by rebels led by the masked man, who turned out to be the queen's virtuous sister.

The stories, if such they could be called, appeared to have replicated themselves, like androids building androids, or golems finally escaped from human control. It was here—in the midst of this fever dream bearing almost no trace of a controlling intelligence, wedged between the hurling of papier-mâché boulders and bump-and-grind floor shows concocted for the amusement of the queen of Carthage—that the otherness of language made itself nakedly and helplessly apparent. The robot tones of the dubbed voices brought out the alien quality of words. The words were still there—the actors said "sky" and "mercy" and "understand"—but they had been waylaid, ripped brutally from the network of communication in which they had once functioned.

A sitcom lost in space might sound like that, tuned in by an inhabitant of Sirius light-years after the destruction of Earth. The context made almost any statement seem as eerily misdirected as the unanticipated threats and sarcasms blurted out by a mad ventriloquist's dummy. "At times your genius frightens me, Archimedes." "I thought nymphs existed only in mythology!'' ''Why did I survive my defeat?'' ''We must be ready to sacrifice all that belongs to us.'' ''I have serious reasons for disturbing your isolation.'' ''Now that Hercules has saved the queen from death, our whole perspective has changed.'' A speech at the mercy of random lip movements, unable to deviate from an imposed syntax, articulated a free-floating cosmic dread. Significant portions of the landscape lay under a curse. Or as Jayne Mansfield put it in *The Loves of Hercules,* ''My people fear the wrath of the gods more than the anger of men.''

It was the peculiar way that the West ended. *Seven Against Thebes, The Aeneid, The Odyssey,* Omphale, the Sabine women, Romulus and Remus, Mutius Scaevola, Coriolanus: it was the last time they would be filmed, not to enlighten an audience presumed to be ignorant and uncaring, but because the cultivated scenarists were running out of stories. As the sword-and-sandal cycle ran its course they grabbed whatever raw material came to hand, Tacitus and Captain Marvel, Sophocles and the Bible and Mandrake the Magician, Tiresias and the Sibyl, vampires and virgins and an endless horde of raucous men-at-arms. The contents of an old cupboard full of irreplaceable artifacts were being briefly held up to the light—for the delectation of uncomprehending inheritors momentarily amused by gold leaf or a bit of fine carving—before being discarded. All periods of history collapsed into one, enabling Hercules and Ulysses to wash up on the Gaza coast and encounter Samson. It was the final garage sale of Thrace and Carthage and Byzantium.

The assembly-line workers raked through what survived of the common fund of imagination, the ragged end-pieces of

myth and fairy tale, threw in some magic potion, some crucifixion, some winged goddess, some sacrificial maiden, some
blind old wise man muttering prophecies to Mr. Universe
1958. There would be no more local languages with their
ancient associations and pungent proverbs, there would be
only the generic dialect of those indistinguishable dubbed
voices: "Hey, Hercules, throw me a spear!" It was a documentary about the party after the funeral. The spectator inhabited that same Atlantis whose magic decayed upon contact
with air, whose systems of security and ritual foundered while
its dark-eyed blighted queen Antinea (Fay Spain in *Hercules and
the Captive Women*) murmured in sonorous post-synchronese:
"I have never told you the truth, because truth and death have
the same meaning for me."

AFTER THEY HAD used up everything in the closet of the
ancestors, they had to find new stuff to display. The theme of
Italian commercial cinema became haste itself, the haste with
which they spliced their found materials together. In an explosion of minigenres the industry annulled any possible distinction between the beautiful and the corrupt by perfecting an
ultrarefined tawdriness, a cinema of poetic cruelty whose
practitioners (Mario Bava, Vittorio Cottafavi, Riccardo Freda,
Antonio Margheriti, Sergio Corbucci, Dario Argento) would
turn out to have been the authentic inventors of the post-
postmodern movie: authentic because they invented nothing,
because they stole from their own movies, because they were
unable to stop obsessively tacking together a recycled dub of
a dub of some archaic internalized European narrative.

It happened too fast to track. First there were just Hercules movies. Then there were Maciste movies, Samson movies, Ursus movies, Goliath movies, and, in the wake of *Spartacus,* a steady putter of gladiator movies (*The Gladiator of Rome, The Two Gladiators, The Ultimate Gladiator*) and slave movies (*The Slave, Revolt of the Slaves, Seven Slaves Against Rome*). The wardrobe department wasn't restricted to togas and breastplates; they could also outfit pirates (*Morgan the Pirate, Musketeers of the Sea*), Vikings (*Fury of the Vikings, The Last of the Vikings*), marauders from the Central Asian steppes (*The Mongols, Maciste in the Hell of Genghis Khan, The Mighty Khan*), Arabian Nights characters (*The Thief of Baghdad*), medieval warriors (*The Revenge of Ivanhoe*), Renaissance avengers (*The Seventh Sword*). There were jungle adventures whose casts and crews seemed rapt in a deep trance imparted by the forbidden jewel of the goddess (*The Mountain of Light, Mysteries of the Black Jungle*), and there was even a series of literary adaptations set in the East Indies, based on the adventure novels of Emilio Salgari, a writer whose classic status was apparently unappreciated outside of Italy: *The Pirates of Malaysia, Sandokan Against the Leopard of Sarawak, Sandokan to the Rescue.*

At the opposite extreme from these fantasies were the pioneering gross-out documentaries of which *Mondo Cane* was the most visible: geek shows for global rubberneckers drawn to the scene of any accident, mixing farce, evisceration, and mood music. A variant form of realism offered canned erotica from the striptease parlors of the Western world (*World by Night, Forbidden Venus, Sexy Proibito*): a genre as much about money as sex, promising admission by remote control to otherwise prohibitively expensive clipjoints. (''You'd have to fly

to Beirut to see this!'') The art of the tease was further perfected in multi-episode sex comedies intended mostly for local
consumption: *These Mad, Mad, Mad Women, Let's Talk About
Women, Woman Is a Wonderful Thing.*

Foreigners were more likely to see the movies which
wanted to pass for foreign, imitations of every variety of
American drive-in product featuring genuine imitation American names like Sterling Roland, Fred Wilson, and Tony Big-
house. For a time these were apt to be James Bond imitations,
as the primal texts of *Dr. No* and *The Ipcress File* were reworked
into *That Man from Istanbul, Our Men in Bagdad, Super Seven
Calling Cairo, Requiem for a Secret Agent, Secret Agent Fireball,* and
other items evoking the experience of reading an Italian comic
book translated into Basic English by a robot with defective
wiring.

These merged almost imperceptibly with the intergalactic
conspiracy theories propounded by a series of backlot science-
fiction thrillers: *Wild, Wild Planet, War of the Planets, Planet of the
Vampires.* Swirling poisonous mists achieved with the aid of dry
ice and green and purple gelatin filters, androids in Op Art
leotards, and the usual banks of beeping and blinking switch-
boards. The poverty of the devices seemed prophetic of the
real future, which would not be a seamless, lovingly crafted
Stanley Kubrick production but just such a makeshift knockoff,
an international coproduction rigged by a monopoly called
United Corporations, decorating the threadbare interiors of its
rocket ships with travel posters of Biarritz and Minorca to
remind the hostages of the twenty-first century what Earth had
been like.

When there was hardly any money for production design,

the cheapest set was the inside of the human mind. That was where the Italians went for location shooting of their horror cycle, into the shadow country of Mario Bava's *Black Sunday* and Riccardo Freda's *The Horrible Dr. Hichcock* and Antonio Margheriti's *Castle of Blood.* In place of plots or sets or special effects, the method had the ingenuity of survival techniques devised by castaways or escaped prisoners of war: to infect everything the camera saw with evenly spread anxiety, sprinkling insomnia and hysteria over perfectly ordinary sofas and windows and staircases. What did they need a script for if they had enough bad mood to poison the atmosphere for a whole planet?

It was enough that the camera slide into the dark, that electronically distorted moans emanate from barely visible attics and cellars, that nameless men in masks and overcoats pull out glistening razors, and that the face of Barbara Steele stare into the lens, looking as if a vampire had nearly finished draining it of blood. (Steele's unmistakable face—with its oversized eyes and its curves curiously askew, moving with extraordinary plasticity through minute variations of gathering terror, mad devotion, seductive coercion, and sadistic glee—was itself a special effect.)

The hero of *Castle of Blood* made a bet that he could spend a night in a haunted mansion without dying. Once he got inside, he became the spectator, watching reenactments of ancient seductions and murders, conversing with beautiful ghostly women who had a disconcerting habit of vanishing without warning. The scenes he witnessed were out of sequence, as incoherent as an unedited movie. To watch *Castle of Blood* was to be inside that hapless protagonist's head and dream with him of being inside a Gothic house that seemed all the more immense for being nothing but a collection of shadows and fragments. No story, just a disconnected anthology of ominous movements: a glide along a banister, a coffin lid opening toward the camera, a zoom into the interior of a closet, a hand stretching slowly forward to unlock a door.

That *Castle of Blood* did not contain a single original visual idea, that it jettisoned coherence and explanation and relied solely upon tone and suggestion, was the secret of its effectiveness. As a member of the audience you had made a bet that you could spend a whole ninety minutes in this movie. The horror lay precisely in these being the same old images, the inescapable companions of terminal claustrophobia.

The airless love talk of Barbara Steele told you that your fate was be to be trapped in this very theater, watching *Castle of Blood*—ninety minutes of living death—over and over, as debarred from real experience as the ghosts who inhabited the castle and lured in outsiders so they could feed on them and feel momentarily alive again. As the spectral inhabitants of the castle called out in unison, "We want your blood, Alan, we want your blood," you understood too late that it was indeed *your* blood that had been sought and duly exacted.

No one seemed more aware of this than the director Mario Bava, who became a brand name for a desperate kind of worst-case beauty, a loving attention to the surfaces of *Hercules in the Haunted World*, *Planet of the Vampires*, *Black Sabbath*, *Kill, Baby, Kill!*, *A Hatchet for the Honeymoon*, *Black Sunday*, *Bay of Blood*. Mario Bava (or John Foam, or John Old, as the would-be-American-style credits sometimes called him) made the frame a kind of funerary display, an ornate wreath draped around the death of a loved image. Antique dolls and mechanical toys were arranged with the discreet sensitivity of an experienced funeral home director masquerading as a fashion designer—just as the pointless, compulsively repetitive death rituals of *Blood and Black Lace* masqueraded as episodes in a sprightly psychedelic suspense thriller full of bright colors and lovely fashion models.

As for the fashion designer, the impotent aesthete behind it all, he was of course (in *A Hatchet for the Honeymoon*) the strangely calm lunatic whose narration—after a brief and suitably artistic prelude of Muzak and solarized photo effects under the main titles—opened the film: "My name is John Harrington. I am thirty years old. I am a paranoiac." Inadequate, and sublimely aware of its inadequacy, the movie version of life could only cling to the correctness with which it fulfilled the ritual requirements. These included the mindless bantering dialogue through which a victim flirted with her eventual murderer: "I'm just an ordinary girl. I adore luxury. I'm terribly lazy, and I like to amuse myself doing crazy things." "What kind of things?" "I just turned twenty-three and I've had several lovers."

It was in contrast to the empty worldliness of such talk that the murderer's voice-overs attained a certain austere dignity worthy of the director's studious color effects and almost pedantically beautiful displacements of the camera: "Death exists, I can assure you, and that is what makes life a ridiculous and brief dream." As for the audience's role in all this, it was more or less beside the point. The most discreetly mysterious of authors submerged himself in his images as if it were a species of suicide. You could fully enjoy the movie only by imagining that you had become Mario Bava, and that this was your own dream, your own death.

THAT, FINALLY, WAS what the Italian marketplace could offer: a cut-rate death more brutal than anyone had yet dared to enact. The three hundred or so spaghetti westerns made between 1963 and 1969 were not there to revitalize Hollywood's tradition but to ornament its tombstone with severed ears and tortured mayors and the wreckage of trains blown up by intellectual revolutionaries. Around here the only savages were white men: cowards, con men, torturers, psychos for hire, railroad men with dead eyes. A dissonant little dance balanced Franco Nero striking a match on the boot heel of a hanged man and a machine gun mowing down a village full of women and children, a blast from a harmonica and a German militarist exported to Mexico intoning with philosophical solemnity: "Look at the sun, it resembles a ball of blood." It might have been an illustrated textbook: *The Joy of Derision*.

But by the time that particular virus ran its course the whole world had caught on. Italy discovered that it was just another Spain, just another Philippines, just another Hong Kong, just another America. A final avatar—Dario Argento, with his further explorations of Bava's science of plotless shock and dismemberment—proved that you could be as ugly as you wanted to be as long as you made it beautiful, that any atrocity was splendid if perpetrated in a Milan art gallery ("Look at this one, it's certainly one of the best examples of cosmic art") or if (like the demonic slashings, hangings, and balewire disfigurations of *Suspiria*) it propounded a satisfyingly decorative color scheme. *Suspiria* held out the hope of an escape from story, a dream journey that might have been entitled *Art Deco Goes to Hell, Disco Style,* or *Alice in the Wonderland of the Malefic Undead.* Horror was a drug you swallowed in order to participate in an otherwise incomprehensible festival. You felt as if you'd stayed up all night dancing and chanting among maskers and witch doctors.

The drug finally—in *Terror at the Opera* (1990)—induced only a numbing reminder of now unattainable pleasures. Argento's science of the terrible had nowhere to go except as far as the back of the throat, to show the knife coming through from the outside in close-up. By then the decorative element had been reduced to the standard-issue postmodern bank of video monitors, and when the police interrogated a prime suspect—a director of slasher movies—he replied: "I think it's unwise to use movies as a guide for reality, don't you, Inspector?"

Of course it would never end, because it couldn't. Life had to go on even if it meant devolution into Mafia revenge pictures, low-cost remakes of World War II, kung fu spinoffs, Terence Hill comedies, exorcism movies, barbarian movies, zombie movies, cannibal movies. In a kind of twilight state— as if in homage to the spirit of minimalism and punk—the artisans of Rome served up elegantly monotonous variations on the themes of mutilation and ingestion: *Slave of the Cannibal God, Cannibal Holocaust, Cannibal Apocalypse, Apocalypse Tomorrow, Anthropophagus, Anthropophagus II, Island of the Living Dead, City of the Walking Dead, City of the Living Dead, Zombie Holocaust, Cut and Run, Trap Them and Kill Them, Make Them Die Slowly.*

But you had already anticipated the inevitable downgrading the night your best friend lost faith in the future after watching *The Last Man on Earth*. He hadn't reckoned on what a soul-killer a quick and cheap dose of despair could be, far more effective than the carefully crafted and artistically serious kind. Somehow you knew that even *that* squalid nightmare would at some future date be regarded as a remnant of a more sensitive, more intellectually expansive age. And it came to pass just as the movies had said.

After Vincent Price dies there will be nobody left on the planet except vampires. The space monsters have figured out how to replicate themselves even after apparent annihilation. The old gods are dead, and after their last pitiful incarnation in the shape of post-synched exiles from Muscle Beach they will never be heard from again. The streets belong to fashion-conscious ax murderers choreographed by Dario Argento against a backdrop of blue-and-pink wallpaper: except that by now even the wallpaper has been obscured by the green foam oozing from the mouths of the demons who just popped out of your television set. It's the end of the world and you're getting off on it.

a ticket to hell

As if to get back home, you sniff in the dark after a lost odor. Beyond the immateriality of movie images you hunt for the multilayered residue of the physical world as if it were a dismantled circus: dung, sawdust, sweat seeping into ropes and leotards, spilled liquor, bits of cracked shell, lingering resinous lamp smell, flecks of rouge clinging to powder puffs, oil and burnt cork and strands of horsehair, splintery benches sodden with rain. The mix of aromas that hovered in the divide between spectacle and audience, floating back and forth in a fog larded with stinks and spices, was oppressive and reassuring in the same instant. The nearness of the bodies was confirmed by the whiff that crisscrossed the footlights like the clouds on which gods floated in ancient operas.

Then came the trade-off. The odors of that coarse and intimate world were surrendered in return for colors, physical presence bartered for kaleidoscopic flurries of movement. You could see more than ever before, but you could no longer smell it. Look at the performers, but they couldn't look back; they didn't know you were there. Your gasps and laughter could not sway them, nor could your gathering alienation from the show prod them toward renewed effort. They smiled at an empty space into which they projected their idea of "you"—an idea whose nature you could only guess at, even as you attempted to live up to its expectations.

The blossoms and bonfires and perfumed actors, rampant wheatfields, bayous constructed out of jagged fern fronds and India-ink shadows, satiny monarchical boudoirs, beer gardens enlivened by joyous mobs of singing Bavarians: all had been translated into frigid precise traceries. They were stand-ins, posted for ID purposes only; for everything else, for the breath and substance of it, the viewer was forced to fall back on the powers of memory and make-believe.

"The aroma is always better than the actuality," murmured Walter Slezak in the 1947 thriller *Born to Kill,* but it was an aroma the spectator constructed out of the gleaming Formica of the hash-house counter, the swinging of the screen door, the Reno street scene glimpsed through the window, and the pungent vowels and consonants of Slezak's Viennese accent as it played against the Middle American flatness of his interlocutor.

Except for a few hapless experiments of the late fifties— Mike Todd's mystery-travelogue *Scent of Mystery* in Smell-O-Vision, and the Aromarama documentary *Behind the Great*

Wall—movies were odorless by definition. The theaters themselves compensated to some degree as they filled periodically
with the smells of tobacco, perfume, marijuana, oranges, the
melting residue of chocolate raisins, and a full range of bodily
fluids and exudations. Theatrical managers had waged from the
outset a war against noise and odor, a war whose battles revolved around the rejection of unwashed and uncontrollable
customers, the enforcement of decent behavior by troops of
uniformed ushers, the discouragement of live entertainment
between features in favor of prerecorded short subjects, the
installation of more lights, more ventilation, better carpeting.
Even so, the life in front of the screen—even in a space designed to be as functionally limited as possible—couldn't help
but be more varied and unpredictable than what was projected
upon it.

BUT IT WAS an invisible life. Who knew his fellow spectator?
The watchers in the dark were a community of mute loners,
as if each folding seat were the warped attic from whose
cracked and cobwebbed dormer window the town hermit
peers at the life of the ordinary folks out in the street. Better
to imagine that evil was up there on the screen than at your
elbow; better even to imagine that evil was behind the camera,
writing the script or directing the actors, than that it sat by
your side soaking up the same pictures.

The word had been out since childhood days that the pur-
veyors of film entertainment were rarely what they pretended
to be, and everyone had gotten his share of chills from imagining the subculture of Satanists and mind-control specialists, the

cabals of Beverly Hills sadists, the white slavers and gangsters exerting secret control of the production companies: the flamboyantly corrupt universe only barely suggested by the entertaining perversities of *The Carpetbaggers* and *Valley of the Dolls* and *The Legend of Lylah Clare*. But what about the people in the audience? How would it be if movies bore some trace of the eyes that had watched them, if those gazes left a mark, like the mirror that witnessed murder in *Dead of Night?*

Whose gaze, in that case, would not be implicated? Everyone had been played upon, however fleetingly, by the shifting surfaces of the demon show: the bands of teenagers whose latent vigilantism was stirred up by *Dirty Harry* at a suburban shopping mall, setting loose a wave of murderousness so palpable that the woman who had fled Austria after the Anschluss felt compelled to leave the theater, shaken by the new era that had thrust itself at her . . . the young man who liked to take acid and go see *The Texas Chainsaw Massacre* repeatedly until it was no more than an abstract floral arrangement, a ballet of dynamic forms . . . the thirtyish divorcée knocking back jugs of Mountain Red every night to go with the stacks of splatter movies rented from the corner grocery store: *I Dismember Mama, Basket Case, Maniac, Don't Look in the Basement, Don't Answer the Phone, Don't Go in the House, He Knows You're Alone.* Where was the protective shield that would isolate them from the maniac sitting one row in back in the dark, chuckling and salivating and muttering words of encouragement during the rape scene in *Serpico?*

Or from the cannibal cultists of Matamoros, the ones who abducted and ate an American college student? They had a secret hideous religion, just like in the movies: in fact they found it at the movies, and used as the key element of their initiation rite a cassette of John Schlesinger's voodoo melodrama *The Believers*. Killers had been obsessing on movies since their invention, incorporating into their private rituals everything from *Triumph of the Will* to *The Story of O* to *Taxi Driver*. Major releases from the Third Reich (*Jew Süss, The Eternal Jew*) made available by a neofascist mail-order outfit somewhere in Idaho turned up in a hip video store in the East Village on a shelf alongside other campy items like *Satan's Sadists* and *Ilsa, She-Wolf of the SS*. Small children rented videos with titles like *Faces of Death* or *Bizarre Asia*—"These films are sold for educational purposes only"—so they could study at their leisure scenes of torture, execution, and massacre.

Presumably murderers were just as capable of appreciating camera movements or plot twists as anyone else. Hitler probably admired the same extraordinary setups and lighting effects in *Siegfried* and *Kriemhild's Revenge* as all the other fans of Fritz Lang; just as he evinced a thoroughly mainstream taste for the good-natured gusto of *Gunga Din* and *The Lives of a Bengal Lancer*. Goebbels enjoyed *Gone with the Wind;* Saddam Hussein preferred *The Godfather,* screening it over and over; Idi Amin's tastes ran more to the stylized cruelty of Tom and Jerry cartoons. Stalin was particularly fond of cowboy movies; he kept calling for more so he could sit for hours sarcastically diagnosing their ideological failings, like a stoned college student getting off on the badness of *Robot Monster*.

THE TASTE FOR danger, for a flirtation with evil, hovered around movies from the beginning. Part of the attraction of the medium was that it allowed spectators to sate themselves on horrors without fearing contamination. Whatever had been captured for their gaze was really elsewhere, with no risk of anything escaping from the screen into the audience. That lure persisted, even as the film industry exerted itself to make movies safer and safer: cleaning up their content while making the theaters themselves cleaner and more brightly lit, freeing movies from their flea-circus associations in order to pitch them to a more sensitive and respectable clientele. The industry's self-chosen keynote was Ascent: the emergence from the underworld of sideshow attractions in order to attain new heights of emotional uplift, epic sweep, even religious inspiration.

But there were those who from the outset were attracted by a contrary myth of Descent, in which the spectator was not swept away to someplace finer, but rather returned to the dank precincts of an evil at once alien and deeply familiar. It hardly mattered whether the Dark Place was a jungle crawling with alligators, the secret headquarters of an Oriental madman, or the heart of an Egyptian funerary labyrinth: the destination was magnetic, and there would always be a sufficient number willing to be drawn to it half in trance, like the hypnotized Madge Bellamy in *White Zombie* gliding along toward Bela Lugosi's satanic sugar mill. The spectator of horror, like the passing motorist whose neck swiveled by reflex toward a roadside accident, ceded his volition. His secret pleasure lay in savoring the trap in which he had allowed himself to be caught: he could now no longer escape from what was to be displayed.

He was free to participate once again in the unbridled voyeurism of the fairgrounds and carnivals where the earliest movies were shown. The fairground was a home to which films of terror would return repeatedly—in *The Cabinet of Dr. Caligari* and *The Murders in the Rue Morgue, Bluebeard* and *Strangers on a Train*—as if, precisely, to the scene of the crime. It asserted itself offscreen too, in the carnivalesque ballyhoo of producers and distributors, in the unending and unchanging spiel reeled off by the barker standing by the gateway of Avernus: "Witness the most shocking secret rites ever performed!" "The Devil God rises and marks his path with mutilated bodies!" "An entire town bathed in pulsing human blood!" The video box for *Jail Bait* promised: "This movie is so grungy you'll need to take a shower after watching it."

THE CULTURE OF horror, such as it was, inhered as much in ads and promotional gimmicks and spin-off marketing as in movies. Advertising for horror movies rarely emphasized the superior quality of script or acting or production. That would already smack too much of choice, would imply that the consumer made a rational decision. The ads suggested, rather, an obscure imperative. You *must* see the movie. It had been lying in wait for you, a destiny you must confront or else be haunted ever afterwards by residual dread of what you failed to look in the eye. That dread of the movies one had not dared to attend was undoubtedly more potent than any of the terrors that movies could purvey. It bordered on the genuine dread for which the movies substituted their pseudo-dread, just as they established in place of evil a manageable and ultimately lovable travesty: *The Mad Doctor of Market Street, The Beast in the Cellar, Fiend Without a Face.*

The undying fairground huckster sold tickets to the world before movies, the world of live tangible horrors, the world of smells. Only by locating the limits of disgust could the antiseptic, desensitized zone of the screen be brought to life. The horror show depicted precisely what gave off forbidden smells, the smells of blood and rotted bodies and cooked flesh —*Blood Feast, The Corpse Grinders, I Drink Your Blood, Shriek of the Mutilated, Meatcleaver Massacre*—and it was tolerable only because the nose did not actually participate. Microscopically detailed flayings and dismemberings signposted the outer boundary of the sequestered and denatured movie image: beyond this point the organic resumes; odors may be experienced.

It was essential to be convinced that the threat was real. These were no mere movie images: they were shells containing actual dangers, like the wax figurines in *Mystery of the Wax Museum* and *House of Wax* within which were concealed the corpses of murder victims. A favorite publicity stunt of the fifties and sixties was to provide stern admonitions and offers of medical treatment to those unable to bear the spectacle: "Warning! We cannot be responsible if you never sleep again!" (The implicit threat was made explicit by B-horror king William Castle, whose crude gimmicks—spooks on wires, electrified seats—restored to movie theaters the risky atmosphere of an amusement-park fun house.)

The humorous fiction that the purveyor of the entertainment was unable to take responsibility for it, that the cinematic spectacle might at any moment escape from its confines and wreak unpredictable damage, was paralleled by a long series of movie situations: the killer leopard escaping from the

zoo, King Kong breaking free of his chains, or (in the 1986
Italian release *Demons*) monsters emanating from the screen of
the seedy theater where a slasher movie was showing.

BENEATH THE FABLE of the dangerous show lay the somewhat more ominous (because more plausible) fable of the
deranged showman. Certain moments—when the tongue was
ripped out of the throat of a suspected witch, or Amazonian
cannibals subjected tourists to meticulously simulated mutila-
tions—seemed designed to elicit the question "What sort of
human being would make something like that?" It was not the
details that were disturbing so much as the contemplation of
the mentality of the people who had thought them up. The
traveling hypnotist who really does saw his victims in half, the
sculptor who embalms his models, the surgeon in quest of
blood or body parts to restore a lost wife or lover or daughter:
what were these but stylized self-portraits of the unknowable
Z-movie director to whose care one had been committed?

He might be imagined as the sort of carny huckster who in
another era hired Tyrone Power to bite the heads off chickens
in the last reel of *Nightmare Alley*. This archetypal manipulator
would be an exploitation genius spawned by the midway,
reared among grifters and freaks and human embryos pickled
in formaldehyde, a mercurial self-made master of transforma-
tions under whose primary incarnations—bum-check artist,
small-time pimp, storefront swindler—lay a secondary menu
of darker personae: an obsessive voyeur like the crazy bearded
painters whose abstractions were always a prelude to rape and
murder, a corrupt tormentor zeroing in on the innocent and

vulnerable with hawklike precision, or the ringleader of the kind of cult his own movies depicted, hermetic conspiracies dedicated to abduction, brainwashing, and human sacrifice.

How did you get here? All you did was ask where the bus station was, or whether the guy with the pointy beard and the attaché case had change for the cigarette machine. Next thing you knew you were surrounded by beaded curtains, silent women with leather wristbands and shaved eyebrows, and a peculiar incense that gave off dark blue smoke.

YOU HAD BEEN set adrift in a world of European exploitation movies, unstable mixtures of poetry and gothic melodrama and outright pornography—Belgian vampires, Italian cannibals, Spanish sex murderers, hooded inquisitors from Portugal—and now there was no easy way out. They extended in too many directions, like the 1969 movie *Venus in Furs* which interwove random components—of jazz combos, sadomasochistic orgies, stock shots of the Rio carnival and the Blue Mosque in Istanbul, Klaus Kinski wearing a djellaba, and a nude body washed up on a beach—to yield an endlessly unresolved dream.

A trumpeter dug in the sand until he came upon a gleaming trumpet—"I didn't know why I'd buried my horn"—and from that moment was pulled into a vortex of artistic sleaze, defined by inexplicable narrative ellipses, distended zooms, soft-focus dissolves, slow-motion pursuits, red and purple filters, a score by Manfred Mann, and overheated voice-overs by James Darren: "I was trapped in a whirlpool that kept sucking me in deeper and deeper. Where was I going? Why was this happening to me? Why couldn't I fight it?" "Deep in my gut I knew that I was still hooked on Wanda." It hardly mattered anyway, since the last shot seemed to indicate that he'd been dead ever since the movie began.

The film's Spanish director, Jesus Franco—an admirer of Orson Welles and the Marquis de Sade, surrealism, and jazz who frequently worked under such aliases as Clifford Brown, Dave Tough, and James P. Johnson—made so many such films that an entire subculture was required simply to keep track of his activities: *Attack of the Robots, The Awful Dr. Orloff, The Erotic Rites of Frankenstein, Erotikill, Vampyros Lesbos, Sadisterotica, Necronomicon, The Screaming Dead, Maciste Against the Queen of the Amazons, Barbed Wire Dolls, White Cannibal Queen, Intimate Confessions of an Exhibitionist, A Virgin Among the Living Dead, The Sadist of Notre Dame,* and well over a hundred other features. When questioned as to his ultimate intentions, Franco could well reply: "The cinema is not only my livelihood but my life. . . . Cinema is above all imagination, fantasy, the transformation of reality, the creation of imaginary spaces. . . . In movies I look for movies. They don't interest me as a means but as an end."

Then again, to have directed 150 or so features in a little over thirty years might not leave too much time for the contemplation of a life outside of cinema. For him existence might consist entirely of a string of disconnected setups: a demoniac nun seducing her mother superior, or two women conspiring to strangle their mutual male lover with a thick chain in the midst of his orgasm, or a fuzzily artistic pan across the terrace of a Mediterranean villa.

The improvisatory freakishness of such a career spilled over into the devotion with which its serious students tracked down its multilingual variants and alternate titles and repackagings. Somewhere in the Netherlands an independent researcher was cataloguing the discrepancies among all known video and laser-disc editions of Ruggiero Deodato's *Cannibal Holocaust*. You realized, with an emotion between awe and horror, that for everything ever put on film there was, somewhere, a cult, extending its membership hourly through the new global bulletin board of video. Every image had its devotees. For every line of dialogue there was somebody who had memorized it, like an acolyte carrying the words of Thomas à Kempis or Bodhidharma in his head.

WHATEVER CLASSIC STATUS horror films might attain with age, whatever patina of high art attached to the contributions of F. W. Murnau or Carl Dreyer, the genre's real concern was not greatness but badness, of all kinds. The moral badness of its maniacs and mad doctors sought further resonance in various degrees of aesthetic and technical badness. Thriving as it did on a nostalgia for the swamp, horror must continue to suggest impulses beyond domestication, threats (or promises) of a defilement beyond even the most recently demarcated edge.

At its upper levels, the horror movie consorted with notions of the cinematic sublime, and in its broad middle its textures became part of an overall nostalgia for Hollywood in which Bela Lugosi and Boris Karloff mingled sociably with Shirley Temple and Fred Astaire. But in its profoundest reaches it undermined all that, edging—through increasingly unpalatable images of corruption and cannibalism, sacrificial ritual and psychotic rage—toward the possibility of a relation with actual crime: either by depicting it, or fomenting it, or even abetting it.

It began to appear as if the point of the exercise were the search—foredoomed, of course—to locate a nadir, to follow the sideshow as it receded into the depths, uncovering images yet more brutal and incoherent than what came before. The primitive artwork decorating the videocassettes of *Shanty Tramp* and *Bloodthirsty Butchers* and *Human Animals* was an advertisement for atavism, an invitation to crawl into the mouth of a paleolithic cave in search of raw unmediated sensation.

Yet not even the simplistic was allowed to be that simple. The swamp of horror didn't live up to expectations if it wasn't a prelude to a further transformation into something very nearly its opposite: an occult story of lost love regained and primeval harmonies restored. After death, resurrection. If fear was the bass pattern of horror movies, their not always explicit melody was the adoration of the monstrous. (Tod Browning in *Freaks* splintered the boundaries of the genre by embodying horror in actual deformity. He could then reverse the poles by presenting his cast of sideshow attractions—the snake man, the Siamese twins, the radiant pinheads—as the custodians of an otherworldly charm, dancing in pagan innocence within a moonlit glade, divine messengers threatened by the ordinary blind sordidness of the normals. The revenge of the freaks, as they mutilated their betrayer, became something like an act of "tough love.")

The fully achieved horror fantasy was saturated in a vocabulary of metamorphosis: passage through mirrors or sealed doors, the exchange of gems or sacred weapons, the donning or taking off of masks or robes or armor, the reciting of spells to wake the dead or make ghosts or spirits materialize, the peeling away of one face to reveal another, the twinning of a single body, a portrait that speaks, the voice of the dead on the telephone, water that parts to open up a path of dry land, a statue that becomes animate, a weapon that turns against its wielder, animals that turn into people, people that turn into animals. Anything at all, so long as it provided access to the impossible.

Classic horror movies depicted ordinary life as intolerably flat and banal until invaded by the poetry of the demonic. The story was always the same. Life was regulated; a safe and comfortable existence moved forward in predictable mechanistic fashion; then something happened. The bare fact of event was the sum total of horror. How many different things could happen? Not so many that you couldn't, if pressed, make a list of them:

1. You walk into your room and someone who looks exactly like you is sitting smoking a pipe.

2. You're tormented by a desire to kill your uncle, and afterward by the memory of having done it.

3. Strange people—a circus freak accompanied by a psychologist—come to town and threaten your girlfriend.

4. Somebody is going to get revenge for everything—the very existence of the city, the world. He's going to roar and tear down the building blocks of reality.

5. Death is going to kill everybody when they least expect it. Try to escape into a different point in time and he meets you there grinning.

6. When you go away on a journey you're going to get taken over and never be allowed to come home.

7. Or alternatively, in your absence the ship of death will come sailing into the harbor of your hometown and your girl-friend is going to be destroyed.

8. People are going to be possessed by devils, or they're simply going to fall into trances, compelled to steal things from department stores without knowing why they did it, become so estranged that when somebody pricks a needle into their flesh they can't feel it.

9. Or somebody will be wounded so horribly—his face burned, his girlfriend engaged to another person—that he will have to destroy her world to make everything better. He will have to take everybody prisoner, lure them to his subterranean dungeon.

10. Or drain everybody's blood in order to bring beauty back into the world.

It all started with a point of contact, the crossing of a line. Or a bridge, like the one that Jonathan Harker passed over in *Nosferatu* (1922): "And when he had crossed the bridge, the phantoms came to meet him." The filmy border between two worlds—analogous in every way to the border that was the movie screen—blurred and permitted passage. The trespass released poetic apparitions as harbingers: like the image, in *Nosferatu*, of wild horses running about on a desolate hill. The gratuitousness of that beauty (what had a commercial traveler like Harker to do with the skittish energies of wild horses or muted twilight effects?) as always revealed the presence of the demon.

Evil inevitably signaled its presence by the exotically beautiful arrangement of lines, colors, and sounds. In its unsettling way it ordered the world, gave fresh meaning to life. The satanic mass in Edgar Ulmer's *The Black Cat* (1934) was an artistic performance which allowed the rasp of organ music to vibrate against the ultramodernist angles of Boris Karloff's Bauhaus chapel; the human sacrifice which was to complete the rite was barely more than a celebratory flourish.

The malefic was not only lovely but primordial. It gave evidence of its proximity to the origin, the omphalos, by hovering around the scrolls, chants, bracelets, tiaras, and altars of buried civilizations. In *Ganja and Hess* (1973), a sacrificial knife salvaged from the archaic Myrthian culture retained the power to infect the unwary with a vampirism that had evolved out of religious rituals; in *Brides of Dracula* (1960), the vampire-hunter Dr. Van Helsing defined vampirism as "a survival of one of the ancient pagan religions in their struggle against Christianity."

The process of making vampire movies might itself be a remnant of lost ritual. Disused mechanisms of thought with nowhere else to exercise themselves—no longer employable in the mapping of magical correspondences or the extermination of vengeful spirits—persisted, wanly, in the more restricted realm of the horror movie. The hack who might once have written a treatise on demonology now wrote the scenario for an exorcism picture.

The scenario that he concocted, or dreamed, or received through mediumistic dictation, scraped at a buried door leading to forbidden realms of savage mythology: human sacrifice, the immolation of children, voluntary castration, sacred prostitution, prophetic schizophrenics, hermaphrodites climbing down through the smoke hole. The horror movies of Hong Kong, for instance, could still remember how superstition imagined the world, with their long-dead spirits popping out of the ground like comical phalluses, their geysers of blood bursting from eyes and knees, their worms and lizards crawling out of the pores of the accursed. You wanted the roots of the religious imagination? You wanted Sumer, Crete, Carthage, the Shang dynasty, the empire of the Aztecs? Here it was in your face, blood and chewed-up flesh tumbling from its maw.

In *Brides of Dracula* the newly created vampire forcing her way out of her grave was urged on by an old peasant woman shouting ''Push! Push! Push!'' as if assisting at a birth. By the same token the stake driven through the vampire's heart was ''an act of healing.'' In an intuitive reenactment of ceremonies whose occasions had long since been forgotten, the boil of evil symbolized by a corrupt heart was lanced, and the site of *miasma,* of ritual pollution, was cleansed by fire or decapitation.

Archaic was by the same token futuristic. The serial killer adopted the logic of the sacrificial priest or the hunter of heretics, creating a flower world or terrestrial paradise out of flayed skin and carved bones arranged in efflorescent mandalic displays. The computer network became animate, buzzing with a newly resynthesized malevolence that rippled through its circuitry like the earth-forming breath of Ra or Baal. The vaginal cassette drive that opened in James Woods's belly in *Videodrome,* the intrusive race of double-sexed extraterrestrials in *God Told Me To* had come to restore the polymorphous mythology of the elder days.

THE PURE HORROR movie would be that in which the forces of evil succeeded in taking over, the one they would themselves direct: pure, and therefore unrealizable. Carmilla, the gorgeous undead girl (invented by Joseph Sheridan Le Fanu) who infiltrated bourgeois households in *Blood and Roses* and *The Vampire Lovers,* was the advance agent for a New Order, but you would never get to see what sort of a world that would be. There would never be *The Last Man on Earth II,* detailing what happened on virus-ridden Earth in the aftermath of Sidney Salkow's unforgettably downbeat 1964 production, after there was no one left except vampires. The inheritors, in such a scenario, would propose a ravenous alternative dispensation, in which the lords of chaos in their unrestrained domesticity could give themselves over to a voracity without end.

But the audience would have to remain content with the uneasy twin of that unmakable movie, the one whose good characters forestalled the triumph of horror. Dr. Van Helsing and his sort stemmed the takeover, slammed the door shut, burned the house or the parchment or the ghoul. The virtuous warriors who kept evil at bay were tolerable only because structurally necessary: no way to define night without at least a perfunctory acknowledgment of day.

Since they could never quite inhabit a universe in their own image, the evil forces were doomed in the end to melancholy and frustration. They longed as vainly for the paradise of the damned as their victims did for a world without monsters. The fresh blood of the living—the legal tender of horror's transactions—was both a provocation and a reminder of inevitable disappointment. When (in the Italian *Castle of Blood*) the hapless hero, keeping vigil in a haunted mansion on a dare, finally gave up his blood to the fawning erotic ghosts with whom he had passed the night, he could not even thereby make them truly alive. They could only make him dead, one of them-selves. An unsatisfying substitution, with which neither the dead nor the living could be satisfied. In that light the horror movie was a miracle play in which the miracle could never quite be accomplished.

Did the eternally aged Dracula end up alone with his mem-ories, watching old vampire movies like a retired general watching and in the end half believing the Hollywood version of World War II? He surely had endless time to kill, just like the child who through interminable meditation on old horror movies began to collect a lifetime's supply of cherished im-ages. The man-made monster, the werewolf, the vampire: they were all alike unkillable. Their persistence might be taken as the emblem of something very like vitality, but *other*.

Dracula figured, in the iconography of horror, as ultimate cornucopia, an infinitely fertile image that never stopped en-gendering retellings and variations and resurrections. Odd that the most inexhaustible image should be that of the creature who exhausts, who drains. He was the god of a religion devoid of both hope and faith, offering not the resurrection and the life, but unending life-in-death, neither sleeping nor waking, a perennial trance of not quite satisfied desire. Unlike the god who offered the waters of life—and perhaps in covert sugges-tion of how unexpectedly hideous it might prove if the doc-trine of the body's resurrection were literally true—Dracula promised the ambivalent pleasures of an eternally prolonged thirst.

ONE OF THE implicit terrors of endless life was the endless recurrence of the same sequence of events. In horror movies the script itself generally behaved as if under such a curse, doomed to repetition and reenactment as the price of having the genre exist at all. It must be unoriginal or die. Horror was definitively antidramatic; the notion of conflict was alien to it, and the only question was how slowly or quickly the inevitable episodes would come around. Its phases were as fixed as the Stations of the Cross.

The group would allow itself to be split up, the characters would go back into the house, would walk into the darkened room. The informed scientist or therapist or psychic would spell out the threat and yet the others would laugh and look bored and idly read aloud the forbidden papyrus. Those who had to die would die, even if they sometimes took their time about it. Everything had to come back, not least the regularly recurring body of the victim, the legs swinging at the back of the closet, the decapitated head tucked away in the drawer, the half-rotted cadaver clambering upward from the bottom of the cellar stairs, the blanched face fleetingly visible at the window.

Spectator and filmmaker alike were hooked on repetition, just like those movie characters (Humphrey Bogart in *Casablanca*, Dana Andrews in *Laura*, James Stewart in *Vertigo*) stuck on a particular melody or portrait or hair color. Zita Johann flirtatiously teased her archaeologist admirer in *The Mummy*: "Do you have to open graves to find girls to fall in love with?" In this domain the answer all too often was yes. Amorous fetishists—or, for that matter, fixated aficionados of the hor-

ror canon—shared a mania for punctual reenactment with the
satanists who waited for the exact phase of the moon and the
long-awaited calendar year to perform their hideous sacrifice,
or the serial killer condemned endlessly to replicate an ordained dismemberment.

This state of suspension did, however, have its pleasures,
not the least of which was the luxury that the spectator enjoyed of being by turns both victim and executioner. He was
able—indeed, he was virtually compelled—to squirm out of
narrow situations by switching identities, to escape from being
the victim by becoming the murderer, to escape from being
the monster by becoming the monster-slayer.

The mind didn't need to know why the masked people
perpetrated their experiments or fulfilled their ancient vows,
didn't require a logic for finding its way around the cellar of
the mad puppeteer, the forest clearing where the full moon
takes effect, or the vault echoing with the screams of the
prematurely buried. It simply settled—with extraordinary relief—into the abandonment of rational pretexts. The pleasure,
as the familiar actions repeated again, was that of a giving way,
an abdication whose visual corollary was the crumbling ma-
sonry and burning rafters of *The Haunted Palace* or *The House of
Usher.* Horror charted a geography of inexperience, a map
requiring almost no knowledge of the outside world. A child
could make such a map, and it was the ritualistic and repetitive
moves of childish thought that horror movies enacted with
such precision. The movie lived in that part of the mind where
magical thinking continued to flourish, and in its refusal to
impart any information whatsoever about the real world had a
curiously consolatory quality.

THE ANTITHESIS OF that cycle of repetition, after all, would be the even more awful prospect of a movie in which nothing ever recurred, and no character once seen was ever seen again: a universe of loose ends, so alive that you could never find a home in it. What could be more horrifying than to be deprived of that core of stability which the horror movie portrayed in exaggerated form as family vault or haunted house, the place from which no one ever departed or was separated?

Here film was finally tomb in the fullest and most literal sense, the graveyard of superannuated motivations, the place where the psychological thriller lost its psychology and where stories went to rot. Except that the obligatory ceremony served to demonstrate at the same time that no story died, that the most threadbare ancient plot—*precisely* the most scrawny and absurd excuse for a reasonable explanation—came back again and again. Here cinema came closest to fulfilling its function of bringing the dead back to life.

Or back to some kind of life: a life which accommodated itself with unnerving ease to substitutes, stand-ins, borrowed dime-store masks. Money or production quality or sincerity or originality mattered hardly at all; as long as the essential actions and gestures were respected, the most impoverished mounting sufficed. Indeed, a certain grainy cheapness added to the harrowing overtones of the events depicted. From the best (Carl Dreyer) to the worst (*She-Demons* or *The Curse of the Aztec Mummy*) the distance was not all that far. The director of *The Screaming Dead* was not mistaken: here—through the window, beyond the door, beyond the cellar—was where the cinema

was no longer a means but an end. The images were so autono-
mous they directed themselves. Correctly performed, the ritual deed preserved the world. The circle was unbroken, just
like that circle in whose midst the demon appeared when
summoned. The dead were resurrected—but only, as it
turned out, to prove that they had been dead to begin with.
The spectator—like the vampire-slayer Dr. Van Helsing, like
the girl who leaped from a second-story window to escape at
the last moment from *The Texas Chainsaw Massacre*—turned out
to be the lone survivor, acknowledging, with more regret than
gratitude, that it was after all only a movie.

the magic cockpit

It was your own war, the War of the Photons.

AT AN INDETERMINABLE moment (it will never be established precisely when the global balance tipped, possibly in the middle of a 3-A.M. showing of *The Brain Eaters*) the recycling of imagery assumed a terminally desperate rhythm. Until then nobody had really believed that the supply of new pictures or new story lines would ever run out, any more than anyone had envisioned a limit to breathable air or potable water. "The fundamental things run dry as time goes by," and even Bogart and Dooley Wilson must eventually end up colorized, laser-ized, and adrift in a soda commercial surrounded by people with spiky hair and Velcro wristbands. The past had just about been strip-mined for all it was worth. As for the present, it had already been exposed as a long-term marketing scheme, existing primarily to provide material for future nostalgia-oriented syndication.

The imagination killers—film, video, all-around media overfarming, abuses of story development analogous to the excessive use of pesticides and chemical fertilizers—had had their way. Impossible to picture anything that had not already been pictured. "They're showing *that* again?" Nothing but old news. Jesus on the Mount? Seen it. Car crash in extreme close-up? Seen it. War, pestilence, genocide? Seen it. The responses—stockpiling of effective narrative devices, replacement of old-fashioned matte work by more fluid computerized imaging techniques, frantic but insufficient effort (too little and too late) to resuscitate dying genres—emphasized rather than resolved an overall sense of closure.

People had nothing left to make pictures of except that very depletion: pictures of people looking at pictures, wearing them, defacing them, combining them, juxtaposing them in allegedly surprising ways, partially painting over them, submerging them in urine, ripping them up and selling the pieces. The pictures wouldn't go away, wouldn't change, wouldn't renew themselves. The opaque icons just accumulated, like the nonbiodegradable plastic jetsam piling up on Pacific atolls. Marilyn, Bogart, JFK, Garbo, Lugosi, Elvis, Duke Wayne, Judy Garland: all were destined finally to be blank marks stirring not even a flicker of response.

YOU HAD BEEN living for some time now in the composite world of *Blade Runner,* a mix-and-match reassortment of elements already in the system. In its exhausted phase culture yielded only Xeroxes of Xeroxes. The real live horses in old cowboy movies had long since been digitalized into software, taken apart, and reassembled like so many molecules cooked in a laboratory to provide food for space-station workers.

By then the people in the scattered, decentered audience had acquired the siege mentality of long-term consumers of spectacles. In the City of Endless Light all corridors were made of movie scenes, like the living-room walls in *Fahrenheit 451*. You looked at thirty-second heavy-metal romances while waiting to get money out of machines. Editing got so fast that the shift from one shot to another was more visible than the shots themselves. Through the miracle of time compression, *Gone with the Wind* or *Wuthering Heights* clocked in at about two minutes forty-seven seconds.

Your destiny was to be the end product of the invention of the incandescent bulb. Night had been abolished. You ate, shopped, and rented videos in BigTown, a full-service urban franchise offering twenty-four-hour cable service and banks of vending machines stocked with a wide range of outstanding consumer products: sodium-free tortilla chips, all-natural soft drinks, condoms, pornographic magazines, and (on a lease-only basis) selected aerobics equipment. (BigTown is a registered trademark of Black Hole Enterprises, a fully licensed subsidiary of the InterGalactica Foundation.) After the harbor lights were rolled up for the evening, you bunked down inside a larger-than-life encephalogram.

A new kind of rerun cycle had kicked in, resembling the scramble device built into compact-disc players, which recombined music in random order. The only game was to guess in what sequence the ingredients would emerge this time, or

how successfully the packagers would pass them off as something new. Prophecy was redefined as the process of betting on
a computerized poker game, putting chips down on the next
big entertainment trend.

Would it be zombie musicals, or teenage Bible movies, or a
nostalgic return to the hot-rod genre of the late fifties? Child
stars singing and dancing disguised as squirrels and rabbits?
Laser discs that you play on your hand? Old movies subjected
to colorization-like processes in which (on a pay-per-view
basis) live actors could be substituted for dead ones, alternate
clothes and hairstyles selected from a limited menu, and eth-
nicity, sexual preferences, and plot resolutions varied upon
request? How about a movie where a yuppie stockbroker dies
in a freak accident and gets reincarnated as a window, every
time somebody looks through it it makes wisecracks, or mists
up if it doesn't want you to see what's going on? Comedy
about a video game with the brain of a fetus, or vice versa?
Adventure movie about commando unit of skateboarders bat-
tling Islamic terrorists in the Poconos? Animated sex movies
about the mating habits of animals, a shrewd and tasteful mix
of Disney and porn? Cable channel that shows whatever movie
you are thinking about? Electric hats that massage your hypo-
thalamus and play music at the same time? The latest breakthrough in microchip technology, a self-programming video
screen implanted in place of your thumbnail, magnifying contact lens optional?

With the lights always on you were less and less aware of
the diurnal cycle. In your new body rhythm it got harder to
remember how long you had been waiting around watching
made-for-cable movies in airport hotel rooms: at Newark a

true crime story about a serial killer, a fashion model, and an abducted child; at Charles de Gaulle a tribute to Gene Tierney featuring exquisitely restored scenes from *Laura, Dragonwyck,* and *The Ghost and Mrs. Muir;* at Narita a soft-core sex fantasy photographed like a shampoo commercial, with ingeniously synthesized orgasmic whimpers substituting for the genitals obscured by artistic floating mist.

O U T T H E R E — O R rather in there, deep inside the wiring— the cyborg world of military computer programmers and security technicians was rumored to have taken over. It happened while your back was turned. A world system had been slapped together while you were watching the decoy action on the 120-channel cable system: a crude trick of distraction— "Look at the birdie" or "Your shoes are on fire"—worthy of Abbott and Costello or the Three Stooges.

The hook was, you didn't want to watch anything on any of the channels so you caught a little of each, shiny new movies about newly defined diseases, escort services, barbarians decked out in mail-order leather gear, nerds on beaches and in locker rooms, reenactments of famous divorce settlements, teen rappers going up against satanic cults—intercut with twenty-four-hour weather reports, protracted infomercials for real-estate scams, diet cults, and phone sex, colorized versions of *My Favorite Brunette* and *Angels with Dirty Faces.* The recurrent nightmare, of running in place and not getting anywhere, gave way to a regime of switching channels at twentieth-of-a-second intervals without perceiving any variation in the visual field.

You had gotten into the habit of keeping half an eye on the screens most of the time. They tracked the world. The nation you lived in consisted of little more than a shared acquaintance with certain murder victims, certain comedians mimicking the behavior of certain television actors, certain endangered animals presented under the auspices of *National Geographic,* certain celebrity tributes and sports events. Somewhere, in the world where things happened, a helicopter was taking off or landing, a body was being unearthed, a man was falling to his death after his bungee cord snapped. Fires were started. States of emergency were declared or denied. The screens told you what time it was, and what time it used to be. They gave advance notice of what you were going to be paying attention to next Wednesday.

What you knew of history came through the screens. Periodically you had your memory jogged by a rapid montage of history's greatest hits: clips of the most memorable earthquakes, plane crashes, invasions, assassinations. Each event had its clip, and finally became its clip—perhaps as much for the people in them as for those only watching them. The watched were also watchers. It made them more real when they acknowledged that they too were part of the audience. President Reagan was just another Clint Eastwood fan. Eventually the ceremony would roll around and the awards would be handed out for best century, best war, best achievement in political manipulation.

The show was not without moments of apparent breakthrough: early hip-hop, or the fall of Communism. It was still possible to believe that air might leak in through a hole in the wall, that styles could be invented without authorization or market research, or that political structures could die a natural death. When students danced on top of the Berlin Wall it was as if new screenplays might actually become conceivable. By the end of the night, after the fortieth instant replay interspersed with anchorman commentary, it had been absorbed seamlessly into the regularly scheduled programming.

The truth that was once sought in location shooting was dribbling away along with the locations. The old-fashioned outward forms of the cities were shells of convenience for fiber-optic communications centers, large-scale data-processing compounds ringed by employee housing. There was nothing to photograph in those wastes of development, nothing even to cast the shadows out of which Orson Welles and Fritz Lang constructed their worlds.

And as for the wilderness which the first cameramen had brought back alive, the jungles and grasslands of true-life adventure, it had been used up while the cameras were otherwise engaged. What had once been called "nature" would be simulated henceforth through a combination of recycled file footage and computer-generated models, achieving an effect something like the artificial gardens of Altair-IV in *Forbidden Planet,* swarming with thought-projected animals. The difference would hardly be noticed if the shots changed fast enough to keep pace with the global Coca-Cola commercial.

It was curious to realize that you could no longer distinguish readily between reportage and staged footage. It had been an article of faith that you would always be able to, no matter what. In an Italian slasher movie the police chief said: "I urge all citizens to remain calm and report anything suspicious to the police immediately." Switching seconds later to the local news you heard the police chief in the real-life slasher murder announcing: "I am hopefully confident we will identify all the victims by tomorrow morning." By the time the reenactments were ready for airing, the thin line remaining would have been smudged and a minor drug bust would come out looking like a William Friedkin production: *To Live and Die in Schenectady,* the latest episode of *America's Bloodiest Home Videos.*

Back when it was possible to tell fiction from documentary you were already getting suspiciously strident and unmediated messages from imaginary characters, as if in oblique preparation for the time when real people would be delivering imaginary messages. In *Scream and Scream Again* Vincent Price's lecture on the coming era radiated the urgency of a message in a bottle: "You know as well as I do that God is dying all over the world. Man is God now. . . . Overpopulation, pollution, famine, nuclear holocaust, war. This civilization is driving us into the sea of extinction. The keynote is control." And in *Planet of the Vampires* the superintelligent alien explained to the last earthling holdout: "You must become one of us. All you have to do is want to. Just let one of us join you. It will give you this wonderful new complexity." *Videodrome* made it even easier: "All you have to do is hallucinate." Between those two poles of behavior—"The keynote is control" and "All you have to do is hallucinate"—the essential role models for the future were laid down.

Perhaps you should have taken those messages more seriously, as smuggled communiqués from within the fortress, instead of pigeonholing them: "Typical pop paranoia, characteristic of late-sixties espionage and sci-fi thrillers." After all, the mere fact that they had leaked from the interior of the machine indicated a certain fluidity, a certain degree of internal upheaval. Now you found yourself testing the limits of a sequestration which nothing could break through. The circuits were delivering only prerecorded messages.

Not an authentic ad lib in the lot. If there had been you wouldn't have believed it anyway: "It's not real, it's just part of the film within the film." You had already seen *Demons 2* with its monsters surging out of the TV set, and would hardly have been naive to believe someone who started screaming at the camera: "You must believe me! This isn't part of the regular program! Any second now they're going to stop me fr—AAEEAAGHH!"

The Gulf War in that sense served as a milestone in the development of electronic entertainment. In its visible aspect the war resembled the cosmic battles on the early television shows like *Captain Video* and *Tom Corbett, Space Cadet:* battles reduced by budgetary constraints to a succession of abstract blips and flashes on the control panel of a rocket ship. Bursts of light, launched in timely fashion, collided with bursts of light. The enemy dot flared and disappeared, leaving the black screen that signified victory. That rough sketch of cybernetic warfare pointed the way toward the fully programmed Soft-War in which people were annihilated without being killed. The neutron effect: no dead bodies, there just wasn't anything there anymore.

If an event on that scale could seem not to have happened, if its battles could be reduced to video games, if it could be celebrated with a network special resembling nothing so much as a rerun of an old Lawrence Welk show, Omani tank commanders marching down the aisle amid a shower of balloons and confetti—"Will you please give a big round of applause for our coalition partners the United Arab Emirates!"—then the process had progressed much further than you had realized, probably well past the possibility of switching gears.

Did the conversion of the public sphere into a cinematic artifact become complete with the ascension of Ronald Reagan—if that was indeed the certified star of *She's Working Her Way Through College,* and not some lifelike hologram out of a Philip K. Dick novel? The Reagan episode was more likely a phase of some larger and more ancient project. If it had significance it was for the overtness of its testing of the waters. Clearly the project had proved its feasibility and could now advance into more complex procedures. For a long time people had been asking: "Is it science fiction yet?" It was another way of asking when the future started, and the answer was the fulfillment of an old movie title: *It Happened Tomorrow.* You watched the future on the news while continuing to inhabit the past, intact and safe from shelling.

What was that unseen space in which the bombs fell, anyway? Nothing but the desert where nothing ever really happened, the eternally returning backlot sandbox across which the stranded representatives of the Trans-Africa Oil Company wandered half-crazy with thirst in *The Steel Lady* (1953), under the direction of E. A. Dupont, who in another life had made the Expressionist classic *Variety* at UFA, with cinematography by Floyd Crosby, who managed to create glistening sweaty close-ups of Tab Hunter indistinguishable from his work on Murnau's *Tabu* back in 1931. This was where everybody came in the end, this no-man's-land devoid of invention or information, a changeless backdrop appropriate to *Sahara* and *The Lost*

Patrol and *The Last Outpost*. In that spaceless space made of props and stock shots the tired inevitable catastrophe was to be enacted one more time: "Hostile bedouins have us pinned down. Repeat. Hostile bedouins have us pinned down. Mayday! Mayday!"

You watched a war whose soldiers were themselves spectators. It marked the arrival of the era of the magic cockpit. Within that designer war chariot, the warrior of the future would function as a computer hacker, or an inspired musician surrounded by a state-of-the-art bank of synthesizers: user-friendly machines for rearranging landscape and bone structure, for erasing cities and devastating coastal defenses.

If he wasn't busy being that, he could pretend to be that through the miracle of virtual reality, with whose joysticks and goggles he could generate 3-D fantasies of sex and power and annihilation. Video simulations functioned equally well as tools for military instruction or alternate recreational lives for civilians with time on their hands. The instant gratification toward which the spectatorship project had been tending all along was now within reach. If camcorders had opened the possibility of homemade porn, virtual fantasy went further and dispensed with bodies altogether, preferring to conjure them up out of a digital library of limbs and cries.

Like the recordings of the sound of the ocean sold for their uniquely tranquilizing effect, the cries could be raised to extraordinarily high decibel levels without causing discomfort, thus blocking out any unwanted background noise. No intrusions would interrupt a private world whose coordinates were as malleable as those of an animated movie. Mankind triumphed over the limitations of the body by learning how to inhabit a three-dimensional Bugs Bunny cartoon.

You must have dreamt it, it didn't happen yet, it was only a movie. People still had bodies: you could deduce that much from the surflike surges of honks and shouts still audible out there where the real begins.

dream sequence

You know you finally fell asleep because you're dreaming.

The dream is extraordinarily well directed—"superbly crafted," as a newspaper critic would put it. It has something to do with going to the movies.

Just as movies have their dream sequences, dreams have their movie sequences. Often you find yourself watching a recently opened movie, and discover it to be richer and stranger than expected. "I had no idea that *Mystic Pizza* took place on Neptune." In any event it is being screened for the first time, as if the dreamer finally saw the "real" movie, the hidden movie: so that *Breakfast at Tiffany's* is revealed as an erotic tragedy in which King Lear, looking like Santa Claus in drag, stumbles across a bloody stubbled heath while simulta-

neously (through the magic of superimposition) witty estranged lovers (Fred Astaire and Brigitte Helm) drift death-
ward in a gondola heading toward the open sea.

These are the most extended of dreams, the richest in plot
complications, open-ended serials where the distinction between the real and filmed is finally dissolved, where your
next-door neighbor turns out to be Eric Blore, blandly discuss-
ing the Balkan crisis in his best comic-butler mode, and your
unwritten love letters are subtitled in both Chinese and English to the accompaniment of an Ennio Morricone soundtrack: jew's harp, electric guitar, and a solitary whistler.

As for their technique, it is impeccable. The sleeping brain
knows all there is to be known about camera movements,
intercutting, matte effects. Not John Ford or David Lean or
William Wyler ever achieved such seamless editing. The fugitive faces are sculpted with a gauzy glamor beyond even those
tricks of light and shadow that once accentuated the cheek-
bones and eyelashes of Dietrich and Garbo. It turns out that
the sleeping brain can duplicate—and surpass—any effect the
waking eyes have ever seen projected. For some unfathomable
purpose it has all been stored in a hitherto unsuspected style
bank.

IT's AS IF somebody fell into a dream in which he was able
forcibly to prevent himself from waking. The dreaming self
would once and for all assert sovereignty: "Nobody's leaving
this room." In this dream the participants would film each
other and watch the rushes. The dream would become a loop
in which the same sequences recurred without variation. Or

so it would appear to the dream-spectators. They would have no way of checking whether it was really so other than to watch those intrinsically unreliable rushes, which claimed to be the same even when they seemed altogether and disturbingly different.

The spectators would be haunted from time to time by memories—so shapeless as to be incapable of articulation—of a world beyond sleep: even if they could not define it with even that much precision, since the notion of "sleep" was necessarily alien to them. They continued to believe that they were awake.

After Chuang Tzu dreamed of being a butterfly, he couldn't say for sure that he was not after all a butterfly dreaming he was Chuang Tzu. The dream movies join up at the edges with those movies that take on the qualities of a waking dream. That could be any movie, since there wasn't one which might not unexpectedly trigger a preternatural mixture of alertness and alienation, the telltale symptom of what could be called movie mysticism, an experience bearing the same relation to religious experience that movies bear to life.

This new brand of religious experience entailed neither a permanent change of consciousness, nor a particular belief system, nor a prescribed code of conduct. It did not even require you to believe that it had in fact occurred, any more than you believed that Olivia de Havilland and her evil twin in *The Dark Mirror* were really two separate people or that Edward G. Robinson had really only dreamt what happened between him and Joan Bennett in *The Woman in the Window*. It boiled down to little more than a fleeting sense of abrupt and inexplicable dislocation: "In what world am I watching this?"

Watch them often enough and it was bound to happen sooner or later. Not necessarily where intended, where a director had programmed just such a jolt—not while watching the exquisite redemptive suffering of Falconetti in Dreyer's *Passion of Joan of Arc* or during the final transcendental crane shot of Mizoguchi's *Sansho the Bailiff*, where blind mother and weeping son gradually became a blurred heap of seaweed on the beach as the camera rose to embrace the ocean—but sweating on a wooden bench in Guayaquil drinking in a flawless Technicolor print of Alexander Korda's *The Thief of Bagdad*.

Years later it would turn out that *The Thief of Bagdad*'s randomness, its peculiar system of interlocking flashbacks and the strange gaps in its plot, were the result of scenes left unfilmed because of the outbreak of World War II. The production had shifted from England to America, from the coast of Devon to the Grand Canyon, and in the process at least four directors had left their mark on it. It was appropriate that precisely those tiny indices of divine forethought that permeated the movie should be entirely aleatory in origin. The moviemakers themselves were only pawns in a larger scheme ordaining that the real and the nonreal should harmoniously come together, and that none was so well suited as Sabu to put the seal on that merger.

The pieces of *The Thief of Bagdad* fit together as they did solely to bring about a sublimely gratuitous scene in which Sabu met God inside a tent in the middle of the Grand Canyon, and God explained that He did not exist. To be more precise, He existed only through Sabu's childish capacity for faith. The movie admitted that it was only a movie, but it was as if the world somehow found a voice in which to stand outside itself long enough to articulate that it was only the world.

You tasted, for once in a lifetime, the full flavor of illusoriness. A long time ago you had fallen into an unreal world and here—just where it became as unreal as it was going to get, right in the middle of *Ursus in the Land of Fire* or *Enchanted Island* or *The Gang's All Here*—the grinning face of Maya winked back at you to acknowledge that none of it had ever really been there. The patterns captured on light-sensitive celluloid were as glimmeringly insubstantial as the patterns refracted through the retina. You contemplated the bubble worlds of *Footlight Parade* or *The Temple of the White Elephants* within a bubble world not all that much larger, and just as apt to pop.

It was for the construction of those micro-bubbles that human intelligence and science had evolved, that savants and engineers and whimsical caricaturists had put together the separate pieces of the great invention. In a roundabout, absurdly elaborated fashion—requiring special-effects laboratories, wagonloads of art directors and prop men, years of systematic alchemical research—the brain had set about creating an image of itself, with a view toward projecting it into every corner of This Island Earth.

Dutiful technicians and creative workers carried out their small pieces of the design, like the laborers on the pyramids. It was as if the technology of movies had from the beginning been built at the behest of an inconceivable Overmind working through human agents, like the alien intelligence that oversaw the recreation in giant vats of its home planet's environment (piece by piece, through the hypnotically controlled labor of uncomprehending British villagers) in *Enemy from Space.* The World-Soul wanted to watch home movies.

Sometime in the year 1521, after reading the *Lives of the Saints,* Ignatius of Loyola experienced a vision of Our Lady and Jesus from which he received ''for a considerable time very great consolation.'' For a considerable time, but not forever: even visions wear off. Every day Our Lady and Jesus grew just a little bit fainter until finally Ignatius had only memory, and then the memory of a memory, in which to have faith.

Instead of having visions modern people see movies, which wear off a good deal faster. Movies eat up images, as each new picture devours those that went before. ''I want that last one again!'' Too late, the train moved on. There goes the back of it. Nothing left but the afterimage of a color scheme or a texture: the bones of the image, a skeletal trace momentarily imprinted on the retina. (It was to illustrate this faculty of cinema that the forensic specialists in Dario Argento's thriller *Four Flies on Grey Velvet* sought to recover from the eyes of a murder victim an impression of the last thing she had seen.)

Film erases memory; video erases even film. ''I saw it once'': is that knowledge, that recollection of a scurrying band of fuzzy shapes retreating as fast as they can move, faster than the Road Runner, burrowing into the inaccessible side pockets of memory as if to hide from an advancing army?

The tenants find themselves in a visual world so full of objects to look at that nothing is visible any longer, as if they had strayed into a gigantic outlet warehouse off the Jersey Turnpike and could no longer find the exit. Once there existed extraordinary precincts—caves, altars, vaults, oratories, plazas, stone circles, sacred groves—with the capacity to become infinitely large, larger even than the world in which they were ostensibly located. In those places silence and darkness were guarded like treasures of inestimable worth.

Now you need movies and television to provide a memory image of such sanctified ground, even if it's only a Steadicam advancing vertiginously through the hyperspace of an intergalactic adventure or a quick helicopter shot of a redwood forest to advertise credit cards or long-distance telephone service. Otherwise the environment consists of phantom space, like the phantom limbs of amputees which they persist in wanting to scratch. Self-sufficient residential compound bounded by guard outposts, multiplex cinema wedged into its slot within an interminable mall at once cavernous and flat: structures containing cubic footage but no space in the old-fashioned sense.

It is precisely in such terminally neutral spaces that, in movies, slasher murders are committed. That is the only way to give them life, if only on the screen. The stab wound becomes a sign of vitality. It's a sort of exoticism, an illusion of massacre to add color to a life that might otherwise seem uninhabited. The very titles of exploitation movies represent a last-ditch looting of whatever reflexive response might be left: *Bloodsucking Freaks, Blood Orgy of the She-Devils, Terror Creatures from Beyond the Grave.*

Night of the Blind Dead, indeed: it has arrived. The lineup of movies at the triplex at the mall hovers aimlessly on the border between being and extinction: *Defending Your Life, A Kiss Before Dying, Mortal Thoughts.* Or, amid the diverse road kill of Highway 82 (a Daily Special of raccoons, groundhogs, small deer) the white plastic sign of a roadside video store beams its wares:

Baby Sitter Is Dead, Shattered, Double Impact, Dying Young, Deer Alert, Nintendo! In the global suburb that stretches from Jersey City to Jakarta, as devoid of landmarks as the Sahel, violence serves as a means of orientation. It's the compass whose bloody needle shows you where you live.

YOU CAN ALMOST remember what memory was. But the recollection already has a secondhand quality about it. It's a rumor, a fable about a world in which there was a past. People stored images and words in their brains. They couldn't look at them; couldn't look them up or play them back; their heads were their hardware. They kept people alive in their brains, made a place for them in a complex landscaped garden called In the Beginning or Formerly or In Ancient Times. By memorizing the lanes and turnings of it—what was planted in what row, where the fountain was, how the seasons altered it—they kept track of everything that had ever existed.

Actually the garden, at its edges, reverted to wilderness. There was no telling whether the creatures who prowled its margins had really existed or had been invented. On those penumbral outer pathways there was a confusion—sometimes sweet, sometimes terrifying—between memory and imagination. But the place was alive, no doubt about that. A writhing forest of neurons was kept constantly busy inventing what had happened—a steady job of maintenance offering unending employment opportunities. Cultures had worked overtime for millennia to sustain by ritual and rote a collection of data that would have fit comfortably on a couple of CD-ROM disks.

After a while there were written documents: stelae, cuneiform rolls, papyri, books. For quite a few thousand years, people assisted memory by writing down markers called words. But considerable mental labor was still required to retain the memories toward which the words could only point. The words were self-evidently abstract, inadequate to do more than suggest. It was an arbitrary system of correspondences by which the known world was translated into actions of the mouth and throat: "When I brush my tongue against the upper palate and then swing it to the back of the lower front teeth, it means sky; if I purse my lips at the same time it means reed." Words were useful tools when you had a fairly exact idea of what someone was talking about—"Pass me the adz" or "Watch out for that falling bucket"—but crude if applied to more diffuse or distant realities.

Explaining the universe and keeping track of everything that happened to everybody was a job that words just weren't equipped to handle. They could memorialize a name but could not say much about who this Robert Jones was that was being memorialized. Basically whatever words said about him could be reduced to: some guy. They might state when and where he had been—in the seventeenth century, in Wales—but then "seventeenth century" and "Wales" were just names too. A name lived in a name at a named time. It's gone now.

At best you could hope for a picture. But before photography most of the pictures from a particular time and place looked pretty much the same. You didn't see an individual but the local standardized technique for drawing lips or eyebrows. You might on the basis of exhaustive comparisons learn a good deal about the eye and wrist of the person who executed the picture—you might even kid yourself that you had an idea what he was thinking about—but not much about what he was looking at.

There were a good many other methods of recording things: maps, musical scores, mechanical diagrams, architectural blueprints, geometric formulas, ledgers of commercial transactions. These things had to be preserved; people had to be taught how to read them; such a process of preservation and training was called civilization. Learning to read the records took so long, unfortunately, that insufficient time was left to consider what they were records *of*. Education consisted of leading someone around a room and pointing out the accumulated records, preparatory to teaching how to read them: "This is where we keep the list of kings—these are the books that the kings liked to read—these are the fields and cities where the kings fought each other—this is the music that was playing in the background."

Memory, as the ultimate in private property, is a vestige of a vanished century. In the new civilization, half the faces in the memory bank are of public personalities, actors playing fictional characters. The farmer plowing his field in the Housatonic Valley in 1803 had how many names in his head? Family, neighbors, people he passed on the road going to and from market, the prosperous and powerful of nearby counties, a certain number of state and national political figures, the characters in the Bible, Washington and Jefferson and other outstanding patriots. He had heard some stories, some ballads, some episodes of history. He may have heard of some actors, some travelers, some outlaws.

But if you went into the street right now and stopped anyone at random you could tap into a knowledge of hundreds, thousands, of familiar strangers: people who do Nike ads, people who present clips from forthcoming summer releases, the aspiring sons and daughters of well-known game-show hosts, people who sold the rights to their murder trial to a famous tabloid. Every single person in the subway station is a walking encyclopedia, a directory of show-biz personalities and celebrity criminals.

They live the consequences of an inner population explosion, a proliferation of internalized three-dimensional holograms. How can they think straight with all those people running around in their heads? And the people in their heads, they too have people in their heads. They talk about nothing else in their all-night talk shows. "I saw him on your show last night talking about seeing her on his show last week." It breeds a nostalgia for the present moment; if only you could really be in the room where you are, laughing along with the laughers in the televised auditorium. They are with you, they are inside you, but you can't make contact with them.

Instead of memory there is the culture of permanent playback. The past hardly needs to be recaptured: it never goes away. The loops go incessantly around until the last possible ounce of sympathy or curiosity has been exhausted. As in the behavior-modification therapy to which the hero of *A Clockwork Orange* was subjected, the rotating images teach the art of numbness.

It's only a movie. Grief at the assassination of Kennedy is assuaged by screening the Zapruder footage repeatedly until it becomes wallpaper. The feelings can be laid out like playing cards. Lust: Marilyn above the subway grating. Anguish: James Dean screaming "I've got the bullets!" They cannot be broken down or digested. They cannot be reinvented the way history could when it was vague and malleable and legendary.

They just persist, like stacks of unwanted mug shots. They end up getting in the way, as if nobody ever died.

The latecomers, the ones drilled since birth in the code of privacy and individual worth, the ones who confidently expect to possess their own "space": they're the ones who find themselves turned inside out, public objects, depersonalized. Or rather they "personalize" their lives much as a ballpoint pen is personalized by having one's initials stamped on it: by a judicious selection of mass products, favorite records, favorite movies, news events that meant a lot. Only to find that tens of thousands of others have made identical selections. Their solitude is wallpapered with clips and trailers.

They try to figure out who they are by making lists of shared memories: types of candy formerly sold in movie theaters ("Remember the dry core of Milk Duds, the soothing blandness of Necco Wafers?"), shows that were on television in 1954, forgotten varieties of boots and cuffs and headgear, bars that no longer exist.

And if memory fails it is all documented anyway. They have been granted miraculous leave to roam inside the image bank, to see anything that was ever recorded. They can purchase films and videos that preserve everything except what they most wanted to preserve. There is no trace of the life that passed in front of the screen. Everything they taped off TV, in order to preserve reality, was a diary from which the diarist was weirdly absent. They can't find any footage of who they are, or were.

SNIPPETS OF WAR and genocide and revolution are dangled and then whisked away: Pearl Harbor, Bataan, El Alamein,

Auschwitz, Hiroshima. Quick flashes, for identification only.
No one would dream of making you actually *look* at it, have
your face thrust so deep into it that you couldn't pull away.
The idea is to get a buzz off how fast the images change. The
music and the editorial quick-step ensure that history moves
forward without ever getting stuck in its disasters.

Until it's as if you were there, in the twentieth century, and
somehow didn't get hurt. Experiencing it was like channel-
hopping on the fiftieth anniversary of Pearl Harbor, bits of
original footage and interviews with veterans interspersed
with *Guadalcanal Diary, The Desert Rats, Victory at Sea, In Harm's
Way,* and the V-J Day scene from *New York, New York.* It passed
by the window—Hitler talking, the Blitz, the beach at Saipan,
the Zero arcing toward the deck of the carrier—and then the
troops came home, to ball games, dance palaces, backyard
barbecues. The last image up had the privilege of burying all
that came before. End it with a smile.

Living in the movie century had been like being invaded by
the wallpaper of the room you inhabited. Except the wallpaper
was a wraparound screen, a music video of unendurable length
whose later episodes frequently incorporated collages or reenactments of earlier material. Keep repeating it's only a
movie, these bodies do but shadows be, it's only a dream
sequence within a dream, and these its actors are like bubbles
which on water swim. It leaves no visible bruises, goes in
cleanly, and passes on noiseless and unseeable.

It was a dream—that ascent, that parade, that fire, that
massacre, that miraculous transmutation of destruction into
fresh flowering—dreamt between the main titles of the Betty
Grable feature and the flickering fadeout of the Charlie Chan
picture on the lower half of the bill. It was a dream, like the

haunted architect's nightmare in *Dead of Night,* the one he woke from each morning only to find it starting up in "real" life, always as if for the first time: so that by the time THE END rolled by it was only another beginning. The people he encountered in the movie—the people he had dreamt of every night of his life—facetiously acknowledged their unreality: "None of us exist at all—we're nothing but characters in Mr. Craig's dream!"

Was it for this you stayed awake until the end of the night, the end of the decade, to bid a long goodbye to the Century of the Eyeball? Flip through the trading cards one more time before the bell rings. Goodbye *Hindenburg* disaster, goodbye Stan and Ollie, goodbye storm troopers of Berlin, goodbye Ingrid Bergman clutching the key to the wine cellar, goodbye bobbysoxers of 1947, goodbye Mr. Magoo, goodbye *Goodbye Again,* goodbye Zapruder footage, goodbye Warren Oates and Jean Seberg, goodbye compilations of compilations of images.

The movie ends. Finally. So the real movie can begin, the one that plays in the dark before sleep. From that fleshly screening everything has been erased that is not terrifying or alluring. The contents of the frame are simplified into their proper and unfilmable mythological proportions. In their divine bodies the stars of the private movie thunder and insinuate, embrace and murder. They were not originally part of the body—they were projected, seen far off, large and external, like fireworks or like the meteor shower that made everybody in the world go blind in *Day of the Triffids*—but now in the dark they have become part of it. They hover about you as they prepare to invade your dream.

IT'S DAWN, THE hour when the vampire Nosferatu is killed, mutated into a transparency by a beam of light coming in through the window. His desire kept him in bed too long.

Dawn, when the Sudanese warriors in *The Four Feathers* prepare to ride down on the British encampment, a dawn that the British commander Ralph Richardson will never see because the Sudanese sun has blinded him.

Dawn, when a bloodied Marlon Brando staggers toward the docks in *On the Waterfront* with swelling Leonard Bernstein orchestrations signifying a new day, the continuation of life, the validity of self-sacrifice and heroism.

Dawn, when in movies about the end of the world a man who has inexplicably survived nuclear explosion or extraterrestrial death beam wakes to find himself alone in a deserted metropolis, and wanders among the monuments and museums calling with gathering hysteria for a fellow creature: "Hey! Where is everybody? Hello! Hello! Can't you hear me? Oh God, why doesn't somebody answer me?"

Dawn, when lovers ride away and escape from every known settlement, the hour when the ending merges with the beginning. "This is where we came in."

You stepped into a bath of light. To write with light was to write on water. Pellucid, each movie showed layers upon layers of other movies underneath it. None existed alone. As in a hall of mirrors they reflected one another endlessly, in a dizzying crossfire of ricocheting forms. A few of the more striking flickers might be singled out and preserved beyond their natural span. Most would fade only to be replaced by others. Your life span was a passage through a palimpsest of water writing, like the waterfall in *Johnny Guitar* through which the outlaws walked to get to their secret hideout.

You knew the pleasure of being perpetually erased by water, of beginning perpetually to look again as if for the first time at the flicker of movement, the beginning of the new episode.

You will never know how things might have been in a different empire.

A ND WILL THIS empire indeed go on forever? Won't the electricity run out, won't the raw materials have to be rationed, won't such practices fall victim to the impending war against pollutants? Won't there be religions of iconoclasts springing up around the globe dedicated to erasing offending images and dismantling the image-making machines, simply in order to make a new start? Wouldn't there be, after the glut of pictures, a deep craving for desertification?

It was peculiar to imagine people three thousand years hence watching *Intolerance* or *Bringing Up Baby* or *Rebel Without a Cause*. By then their criteria would of course have changed drastically. Just as you, watching a thirties movie, already paid less attention to story and jokes than to stray effects of lighting and brief glimpses of period furniture and costume. Those future movie buffs might be fascinated by earlier phases of evolution: vanished nuances of bone structure or nerve reflex, archaic vocal patterns evidently associated with amusement or terror. They would perhaps watch the wonderful comedians as if studying an amoeba under glass.

Or maybe they would simply lose interest. Having evolved

out of a world where the little living pictures were everywhere, perhaps the most exciting thing they could witness would be the screen going blank. The hum of the soundtrack cutting out would announce a healing influx of voluntary silence.

And then what would they do, as they began learning again how to live in a world without movies? What would it then become possible for them to see?

What a world that would be. What stories could be told of it. What a movie it would make.

index of films cited

A Nous la Liberté
1931 France
D: René Clair
C: Raymond Cordy, Henri
   Marchand

Action in the North Atlantic
1943 U.S.
D: Lloyd Bacon
C: Humphrey Bogart, Raymond
   Massey

An Adventure of Salvator Rosa
1939 Italy
D: Alessandro Blasetti
C: Gino Cervi, Luis Ferida

The Adventures of Captain
   Marvel
1941 U.S.
D: William Witney
C: Tom Tyler

The African Lion
1955 U.S.
D: James Algar

Air Force
1943 U.S.
D: Howard Hawks
C: John Garfield, Gig Young

The Arrival of a Train at the La
Ciotat Station
1895 France
D: Louis Lumière

Attack of the Fifty-Ft. Woman
1958 U.S.
D: Nathan Hertz
C: Allison Hayes, William
Hudson

Attack of the Puppet People
1958 U.S.
D: Bert I. Gordon
C: John Agar, John Hoyt

Attack of the Robots
1965 Spain
D: Jess Franco
C: Eddie Constantine, Francois
Brion

Automobile Thieves
1906 U.S.
D: Vitagraph

L'Avventura
1960 Italy
D: Michelangelo Antonioni
C: Monica Vitti, Lea Massari

The Awful Dr. Orloff
1961 Spain
D: Jess Franco
C: Howard Vernon, Diana
Lorys

The Awful Truth
1937 U.S.
D: Leo McCarey
C: Cary Grant, Irene Dunne

Baby Sitter Is Dead
see Don't Tell Mom the Baby
Sitter Is Dead

Back to Bataan
1945 U.S.
D: Edward Dmytryk
C: John Wayne, Anthony
Quinn

The Bad and the Beautiful
1952 U.S.
D: Vincente Minnelli
C: Kirk Douglas, Lana Turner

Bad Day at Black Rock
1955 U.S.
D: John Sturges
C: Spencer Tracy, Robert Ryan

The Badlanders
1958 U.S.
D: Delmer Daves
C: Alan Ladd, Ernest Borgnine

The Band Wagon
1953 U.S.
D: Vincente Minnelli
C: Fred Astaire, Cyd Charisse

La Chienne
1931 France
D: Jean Renoir
C: Michel Simon, Janie Marèze

Chinese Laundry Scene
1894 U.S.
D: Edison

Citizen Kane
1941 U.S.
D: Orson Welles
C: Orson Welles, Joseph
   Cotten

City of the Living Dead
1980 Italy
D: Lucio Fulci
C: Christopher George, Janet
   Agren

City of the Walking Dead
1980 Italy
D: Umberto Lenzi
C: Hugo Stiglitz, Laura Trotter

Cleopatra
1963 U.S.
D: Joseph L. Mankiewicz
C: Elizabeth Taylor, Richard
   Burton

A Clockwork Orange
1971 Great Britain
D: Stanley Kubrick
C: Malcolm McDowell, Patrick
   Magee

Cobra Woman
1944 U.S.
D: Robert Siodmak
C: Maria Montez, Jon Hall

The Cobweb
1955 U.S.
D: Vincente Minnelli
C: Richard Widmark, Gloria
   Grahame

Confessions of a Police Captain
1971 Italy
D: Damiano Damiani
C: Martin Balsam, Franco Nero

Contempt
1963 France
D: Jean-Luc Godard
C: Michel Piccoli, Brigitte
   Bardot

Contract on Cherry Street
1977 U.S.
D: William A. Graham
C: Frank Sinatra, Harry
   Guardino

The Conversation
1974 U.S.
D: Francis Ford Coppola
C: Gene Hackman, John Cazale

8 ½
1963 Italy
D: Federico Fellini
C: Marcello Mastroianni,
   Claudia Cardinale

Endless Advance
1937 Japan
D: Tomu Uchida

Enemy from Space
1957 Great Britain
D: Val Guest
C: Brian Donlevy, Michael
   Ripper

The Erotic Rites of
   Frankenstein
1972 Spain
D: Jess Franco
C: Lina Romay, Howard
   Vernon

Erotikill
1973 France
D: Jess Franco
C: Lina Romay, Monica Swin

Escapade in Japan
1957 U.S.
D: Arthur Lubin
C: Cameron Mitchell, Teresa
   Wright

The Escaped Lunatic
1903 U.S.
D: Biograph

Escape to Burma
1955 U.S.
D: Allan Dwan
C: Barbara Stanwyck, Robert
   Ryan

The Eternal Jew
1940 Germany
D: Fritz Hippler

Everybody Does It
1949 U.S.
D: Edmund Goulding
C: Paul Douglas, Linda Darnell

Executive Action
1973 U.S.
D: David Miller
C: Burt Lancaster, Robert Ryan

Executive Suite
1954 U.S.
D: Robert Wise
C: William Holden, Barbara
   Stanwyck

Fabiola
1947 Italy
D: Alessandro Blasetti
C: Michele Morgan, Michel
   Simon

Fire on That Flag!
1944 Japan

Fire over Africa
1954 U.S.
D: Richard Sale
C: Maureen O'Hara,
   Macdonald Carey

Five Against the House
1955 U.S.
D: Phil Karlson
C: Kim Novak, Guy Madison

The Flame and the Arrow
1950 U.S.
D: Jacques Tourneur
C: Burt Lancaster, Virginia
   Mayo

Flame of the Islands
1955 U.S.
D: Edward Ludwig
C: Yvonne De Carlo, Howard
   Duff

Flaming Feather
1951 U.S.
D: Ray Enright
C: Sterling Hayden, Forrest
   Tucker

Flaming Star
1960 U.S.
D: Don Siegel
C: Elvis Presley, Barbara Eden

Flight to Hong Kong
1956 U.S.
D: Joseph M. Newman
C: Rory Calhoun, Barbara Rush

Flight to Tangier
1953 U.S.
D: Charles Marquis Warren
C: Joan Fontaine, Jack Palance

Flower of Patriotism
1942 Japan

Footlight Parade
1933 U.S.
D: Lloyd Bacon
C: James Cagney, Joan Blondell

For a Few Dollars More
1965 Italy
D: Sergio Leone
C: Clint Eastwood, Lee Van
   Cleef

Forbidden
1953 U.S.
D: Rudolph Maté
C: Tony Curtis, Joanne Dru

Forbidden Planet
1956 U.S.
D: Fred Wilcox
C: Walter Pidgeon, Anne
   Francis

Gold Diggers of 1933
1933 U.S.
D: Mervyn Le Roy
C: Ruby Keeler, Joan Blondell

Gone with the Wind
1939 U.S.
D: Victor Fleming
C: Vivien Leigh, Clark Gable

The Good Earth
1937 U.S.
D: Sidney Franklin
C: Paul Muni, Luise Rainer

Goodbye Again
1961 U.S.
D: Anatole Litvak
C: Ingrid Bergman, Anthony
   Perkins

La Grande Illusion
1937 France
D: Jean Renoir
C: Jean Gabin, Erich von
   Stroheim

Grand Prix
1966 U.S.
D: John Frankenheimer
C: James Garner, Eva Marie
   Saint

The Great Escape
1963 U.S.
D: John Sturges
C: Steve McQueen, James
   Garner

The Great Race
1965 U.S.
D: Blake Edwards
C: Tony Curtis, Jack Lemmon

The Great Train Robbery
1903 U.S.
D: Edwin S. Porter
C: Marie Murray, Bronco Billy
   Anderson

Guadalcanal Diary
1943 U.S.
D: Lewis Seiler
C: Preston Foster, Lloyd Nolan

Gun Crazy
1950 U.S.
D: Joseph H. Lewis
C: Peggy Cummins, John Dall

The Gunfighter
1950 U.S.
D: Henry King
C: Gregory Peck, Helen
   Westcott

House of Madness
1972 Mexico
D: Juan Lopez Moctezuma
C: Claudio Brook, Arturo
Hanse

The House of Usher
1960 U.S.
D: Roger Corman
C: Vincent Price, Mark Damon

House of Wax
1953 U.S.
D: André de Toth
C: Vincent Price, Frank
Lovejoy

How the West Was Won
1962 U.S.
D: Henry Hathaway, George
Marshall & John Ford
C: James Stewart, Debbie
Reynolds

Huk!
1956 U.S.
D: John Barnwell
C: George Montgomery, Mona
Freeman

Human Desire
1954 U.S.
D: Fritz Lang
C: Glenn Ford, Gloria Grahame

Human Wreckage
1923 U.S.
D: John Griffith Wray
C: Mrs. Wallace Reid, George
Hackathorne

The Hunchback of Notre Dame
1939 U.S.
D: William Dieterle
C: Charles Laughton, Maureen
O'Hara

Hypnotist's Revenge
1907 U.S.
D: Joseph A. Golden

I Died a Thousand Times
1955 U.S.
D: Stuart Heisler
C: Jack Palance, Shelley
Winters

I Dismember Mama
1972 U.S.
D: Paul Leder
C: Zooey Hall, Geri Reishl

I Drink Your Blood
1971 U.S.
D: David Durston
C: Jadine Wong, Ronda Fultz

I Married a Monster from
Outer Space
1958 U.S.
D: Gene Fowler, Jr.
C: Tom Tryon, Gloria Talbott

My Son John
1952 U.S.
D: Leo McCarey
C: Robert Walker, Helen
Hayes

The Mysterians
1959 Japan
D: Inoshiro Honda
C: Kenji Sahara, Yumi
Shirakawa

Mysteries of the Black Jungle
1964 Italy
D: Luigi Capuano
C: Guy Madison, Inge Schoner

Mystery of the Wax Museum
1933 U.S.
D: Michael Curtiz
C: Lionel Atwill, Fay Wray

Mystic Pizza
1988 U.S.
D: Donald Petrie
C: Julia Roberts, Annabeth
Gish

Naked Alibi
1954 U.S.
D: Jerry Hopper
C: Sterling Hayden, Gloria
Grahame

The Naked Dawn
1955 U.S.
D: Edgar Ulmer
C: Arthur Kennedy, Betta St.
John

Naked Earth
1958 Great Britain
D: Vincent Sherman
C: Juliette Greco, Richard
Todd

The Naked Edge
1961 U.S.
D: Michael Anderson
C: Gary Cooper, Deborah Kerr

The Naked Hills
1956 U.S.
D: Josef Shaftel
C: David Wayne, Keenan
Wynn

The Naked Jungle
1954 U.S.
D: Byron Haskin
C: Charlton Heston, Eleanor
Parker

The Naked Spur
1953 U.S.
D: Anthony Mann
C: James Stewart, Robert Ryan

You're Never Too Young
1955 U.S.
D: Norman Taurog
C: Dean Martin, Jerry Lewis

Zombie Holocaust
1980 Italy
D: Marino Girolami
C: Ian McCullough, Sherry Buchanan